FOR MY MOM AND DAD

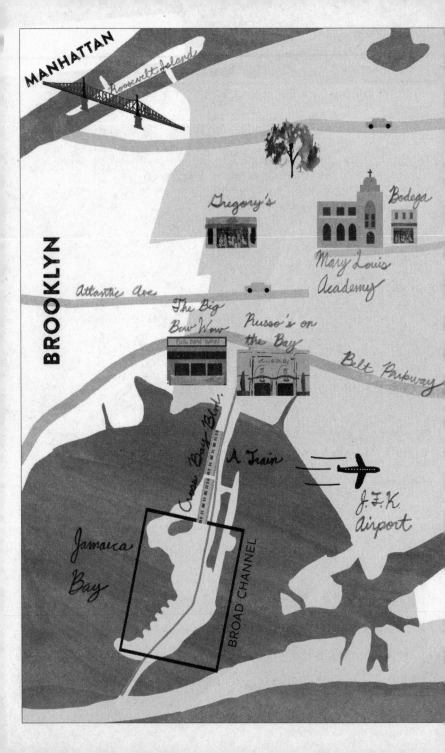

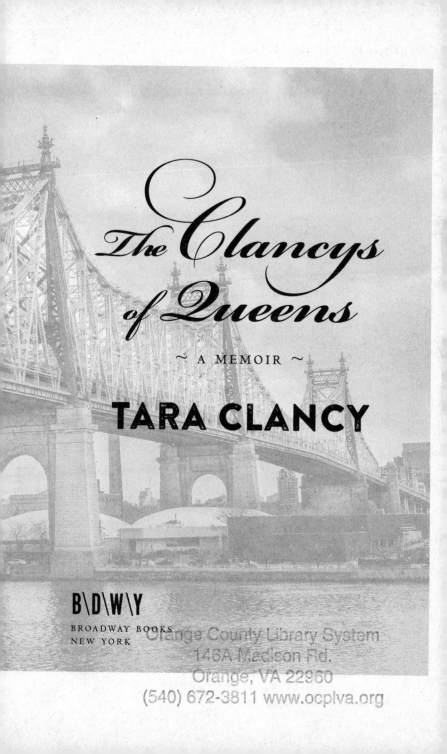

The Clancys of Queens

~ A MEMOIR ~

TARA CLANCY

B\D\W\Y

BROADWAY BOOKS
NEW YORK

Library of Congress Cataloging-in-Publication Data
Names: Clancy, Tara, 1980– author.
Title: The Clancys of Queens : a memoir / Tara Clancy.
Description: First edition. | New York : Crown Publishers, 2016.
Identifiers: LCCN 2016003555 (print) | LCCN 2016020890 (ebook) |
    ISBN 9781101903117 (hardcover) | ISBN 9781101903124 (ebook)
Subjects: LCSH: Clancy, Tara, 1980—Childhood and youth. | Queens
    (New York, N.Y.)—Social life and customs. | New York (N.Y.)—
    Social life and customs. | Clancy, Tara, 1980—Family. | Clancy
    family.
Classification: LCC F128.68.Q4 C57 2016 (print) |
    LCC F128.68.Q4 (ebook) | DDC 974.7/243—dc23
LC record available at https://lccn.loc.gov/2016003555

ISBN 978-1-101-90313-1
Ebook ISBN 978-1-101-90312-4

Printed in the United States of America

Cover design: Kristen Haff
Cover photographs: (photo) courtesy of the author;
(baseball) marcos77/E+ / Getty Images
Frontispiece photograph: Nick Starichenko/Shutterstock
Map and bridge illustrations: Jon Han

10 9 8 7 6 5 4 3 2 1

First Paperback Edition

I'm the whirling dervish of Queens, spinning around and around, arms flapping, my father's boxing gloves like cinder blocks strapped to my seven-year-old hands. With a single left hook, Tommy O'Reilly, my best friend, has just knocked me blind. But the goddamn gloves are so heavy, I can't even lift them, so, unable to punch or see, I start flapping and spinning, gaining speed as I go, praying the added centrifugal force will do the trick—and if science fails me, at least I'll look so nuts that maybe he won't try again.

The ring is our front yard, a splotch of grass split in half by a cement path and hemmed by a short and shabby chain-link fence that surrounds both of our houses: mine looks exactly like a single-wide trailer, but it's actually a converted former boat shed that sits in front of Tommy's proper two-story Colonial. The whole setup is like some modern-day feudal arrangement, except instead of a lord and lady, there's the O'Reillys. And instead of it being medieval Europe, it's Broad Channel, Queens, 1987.

I live in the shed with my father—I am a first-grader, he is a cop, and we are the serfs. For the past five years my dad has lived in the O'Reillys' old boat shed because it was the first place in his hometown he could find, and afford, after my parents' divorce.

I spend every other weekend there with him, and we have a routine. We share the pullout couch, and after he falls asleep, I crawl out from the crook of his back to the end of the bed and turn up the heat on our electric blanket. In the morning he tells me not to do it again.

Because there is nowhere to go when we get out of bed, we don't. Instead, first thing in the morning he turns his tube socks into puppets called Filbert and Albert, who are mute and whose only shtick is fighting and making up. My dad can keep them going for close to an hour.

Eventually we have our breakfast and go to Mass, and then I spend the rest of the day playing with Tommy

O'Reilly. Every so often "playing" just means trying to punch each other in the face.

Broad Channel is a bread crumb of an island between Howard Beach and Rockaway, with a single through street, Cross Bay Boulevard, and cross streets that dead-end at the water. Far off in the distance you can see Manhattan, its familiar miniature metal geometry in a strange frame of fog and reeds.

We've got no supermarket, high school, pharmacy, or library. Almost everything is on the other side of the bridges at either end of our town. For better or worse, we are 2,500-odd people adrift in Jamaica Bay, untethered from the rest of the world. Really. No poetics intended—despite being in Queens, Broad Channel isn't even connected to the New York City sewage lines. Instead, we have septic tanks. Even our shit can't escape.

Most people here are Irish Catholic, so we do have more than our share of bars and a church, St. Virgilius. My dad was an altar boy there and has been a devout Catholic ever since. In fact, becoming a cop was his second-choice career. His first was to be a priest. He even went into the seminary, fervently hoping God would call him. As it turns out, He didn't. My dad left with no hard feelings and soon afterward discovered that, while he wasn't cut out for bringing God's love to the masses, he was just great at throwing them in jail. He became a warrant-squad cop, which is basically a bounty hunter for the NYPD.

In addition to our bars and church, Broad Channel has two corner stores, one owned by Mr. and Mrs. Kroog and the other owned by Kim. We call them Kroogs' and Kim's, which may or may not be the actual names of the stores.

I love Kroogs' because, together with the typical candy and chips, the store also sells all the old '50s-era toys: jacks, yo-yos, and those paddles with a rubber ball attached by string—the kinds of toys kids never have a hard time getting their dads to buy.

Kim is a friend of ours and the sum total of Broad Channel's ethnic diversity. Since I turned seven, my dad has been letting me walk the three blocks from our house to Kim's, alone, to get us our snacks: Yankee Doodles for him and a twenty-five-cent bag of BBQ potato chips for me. But Dad tells me I have to walk up Cross Bay to get there, not along the more desolate Shad Creek Road, where we live. The *one* time he caught me taking the unapproved route, I was grounded. (In our little house, which has only one room, that meant being banished to the couch.)

That particular time I sat there mouthing, "I hate you. I hate you. I hate you."

Finally, Dad yelled, "Stop that, will ya?!"

"I'm calling the police!" I said, naturally.

He cracked up, then looked me dead in the eye and said, "I AM the police."

My jaw dropped. Sure, I knew he was *a* cop, but in that moment, I really believed he was *all* cops, like some sci-fi supreme omniscient cloned being. I sat in stunned silence for the remainder of my banishment.

Beyond our bars, church, and corner stores, Broad Channel also boasts not one but two veterans' halls. But if you had called either of them "the veterans' hall," I wouldn't have known what you meant. To me they're "the VFW," which is nothing more than a place you go for a party. And no matter whose party it is or what it's for, there will be aluminum trays of Swedish meatballs and baked ziti, giant plastic tubs of potato and macaroni salads, bowls of potato chips, and cans of beer. And music playing from a boom box. The smaller of the two VFWs is an arm's length from our little house, and by 9:00 p.m. on a Friday or Saturday, without fail, Bruce Springsteen's "Bobby Jean" comes blaring through our walls. But you never complain about the Boss.

Broad Channel has boats, too—lots of old rickety

ones and a handful of sleek, fast ones. And whether you have a boat to moor or not, most waterfront houses have long wooden docks extending from their back doors into the bay. On summer days we kids spend hours fishing off the docks or swimming in the bay or tumbling down the dunes. But this is not that kind of day. Today, instead of doing any of those lovely things, we are boxing ourselves blind.

Unable to stave Tommy off, in addition to my spinning and flapping I start to scream, "I can't see! I can't seeeee!!" And then I hear his feet come to a stop. Jimmy and Richie O'Reilly, his brother and cousin, are our only spectators. Up until this point they have been chanting, "Fight! Fight! Fight!" But even they go quiet. Then Richie, who is the *Peanuts* character Linus come to life, leans in to me and asks, "Ya okay, Tara?"

I stop spinning and scream, "I'm blind, goddamnit!!!"

Around the time Tommy punched me in the face, the stretch limousine on its way to pick me up at my little house would have just exited the Belt Parkway. As I started my flapping and spinning, it would have been cruising down Cross Bay through the Italian stronghold of Howard Beach. I imagine a couple of guys in sweat suits and white leather slip-on Keds peering over their cigars at the limo, wondering, "Who's gettin' married?" Or, "Prom already?" But they probably weren't thinking, "Betcha that limo is going to pick up the Channel Rat Clancy girl who just got her lights knocked out on her front lawn."

Either way, after passing Gold's Gym, Vincent's Clam Bar, and Russo's on the Bay, perhaps at the very moment I screamed "I'm blind, goddamnit," that limo would have been nearing the last major landmark you hit before the bridge to Broad Channel, the Big Bow Wow.

There's a chance, if the limo wasn't coming to get me, that Dad and I would have gone there that night. As always, we'd have slid into one of the Bow Wow's burnt-orange Formica booths and scarfed down their famous hot roast beef sandwiches before the bread got too soggy and fell apart in our fingers. Afterward, we'd go into their arcade to play Skee-Ball. As usual, my father would dance around on his tiptoes like Fred Flintstone before flamboyantly drawing back his arm and firing a ball up the lane. But there wasn't gonna be any Skee-Ball showdowns or steaming sandwiches today.

As the limousine climbed over the bridge to Broad Channel, the driver might have the A train chugging along on his left, crossing its own bridge toward the end of the line. To his right would stretch the wide expanse of Jamaica Bay, toy-size boats bobbing amid swirls of marsh in front of the very distant tail end of Manhattan—snapshot perfection for all of three seconds.

When you reach Broad Channel, there is nothing on either side but green for a mile-long stretch on Cross Bay—the Jamaica Bay Wildlife Refuge, a national park and bird sanctuary. As you drive past, you might see a wild turkey or a birder with binoculars or an enormous osprey with a fish dangling from its beak flying inches above the windshield of some guy's Oldsmobile. More typically, though, you don't see any people or rare birds—just a pleasant, mile-long patch of woods, immediately followed by toilets.

Rows and rows of blue plastic Porta Potties mark the end of the beautiful national park and the start of our town. It's the headquarters of the Call-A-Head Corporation, our most profitable locally owned business. And, after seeing the Porta Potties themselves, you come upon a sign with their motto: CALL-A-HEAD, WE'RE NUMBER 1 AT PICKING UP NUMBER 2!

After that genius bit of marketing, there are just rows of

homes—a mix of battered clapboard shanties and sprawling, bay-windowed beauties. Ours is on Shad Creek Road,
a slanted little street just past a lot filled with abandoned
cars, among them my dad's rusted, long-dead, yellow '74
Volkswagen Karmann Ghia.

Our home is by far the smallest in town, and when the
driver pulls up out front, the house and the limo aren't
much different in size.

Tommy, Jimmy, and Richie stand in silence, staring at
their sneakers, as my dad waves two fingers in front of my
face. My eyes follow them until he unfurrows his brow
and says, "You're just fine now, Scooter." But right before
he walks away, he looks down. Cupping one of my gloved
hands in his, he shakes his head. "No wonder! Jesus, next
time you kids wanna box, we'll getcha kids' gloves—them
things are for practice, sixteen ounces apiece, ya mopes!"

We all shrug. And after a half-second pause, Tommy
says, "So, you wanna go play in the lot?" I smile and take
off running for the gate. But I never make it. Halfway
there I see the limo and stop dead. Jimmy, Richie, and
Tommy pile up behind me. "Damn, Tara, it's already

time?" someone says to my back. I drop my arms to my sides and manage a slow, disappointed nod.

Looking behind me, I see my dad standing in the doorway of our house with my duffel bag. He gives me a hug, "You have fun, Scooter, okay?"

"I wanna stay."

"I know, kiddo. It'll be all right."

The driver opens the door for me, and I climb in.

Out the right window my dad waves, and out the left Tommy, Jimmy, and Richie scale the chain-link fence of the lot.

1

When I twist the mental radio-tuner dial of my memory as far back as it'll go, I get staticky snippets of my parents and me from my earliest days, but that sweet, crystal-clear reception actually first comes in on the time I spent with my grandparents. In other words, as best as I can remember, life begins for me in a tiny ad hoc geriatric Italian village on 251st Street in Bellerose, Queens.

With both my mom and dad working double-time after their divorce, starting at age three I spent the weekdays in the care of my grandma, Rosalie Riccobono, who lived, of course, with my grandpa, Bruno "Ricky" Riccobono, who in turn shared a two-family house with my great-aunt, Mary Zacchio, that just happened to be next door to the homes of two other Italian American septuagenarian couples, Tina and Lenny Curranci, and Anna and Joe Paradise. And though I was with my parents on weeknights and weekends, bouncing between their vastly different worlds, my most vivid early memories are born in this four-hundred-meter stretch of street, in these three abutting houses, with these seven elderly Italians.

In my mind, the scene plays like one continuous Steadicam shot tracking me as I weave my way through side doors to kitchens, down hallways to living rooms, from one house to the next, to the next, casting off hellos left and right, like Henry Hill in the Copacabana in *Goodfellas*. That shot begins when a sharply dressed Ray Liotta hands the keys of his Caddy to the valet on a bustling Manhattan street outside the club and then makes his way inside with the beautiful Lorraine Bracco on his arm. My scene begins with my mother's beat-up blue Oldsmobile screeching to a halt in front of The Geriatrics of 251st Street compound and me, age five, hopping out in a pair of jeans with the knees torn out and an Incredible Hulk backpack.

At the time, 1985, Mom and I still live in the house my parents once shared, ten minutes away in Rosedale, Queens, but she drops me at Grandma's every morning before heading to work. I was in kindergarten at PS 133 in

Bellerose, but on days like this one, when I was off from school, I wasted no time in starting my rounds.

Right after Mom peels out, I leap up Grandma's stoop steps two at a time, yank open the screen door, and head into the kitchen to find my grandpa on his way out to work. In his late fifties, after thirty years of driving a truck for Linens of the Week, he got a job at the Metropolitan Life Insurance Company. And now, at seventy, he still works five days a week, taking great pride in stuffing his barrel chest and thick legs into a perpetually too-tight, brown polyester suit. With his round belly, big bulbous nose, and deep, genuine happiness, Grandpa is as close to Buddha as an Italian-born, Brooklyn-bred, truck-driver-turned-life-insurance-salesman has ever been. When I appear, he is standing at the kitchen sink, displaying his typical toothy grin between blissful gulps of his infamously disgusting breakfast concoction: hunks of rock-hard, stale Italian bread jammed into the bottom of this one particular red-rimmed, white enamel pot, then topped with a couple of cups of sweet, milky coffee and cooked until the whole mess could be eaten with a spoon like porridge. He calls it *zuppe* (soup), which just makes it sound worse, and of his six children and eighteen grandchildren, only he and I don't find it repulsive. "Morning, Shrimpy!" he says, putting the last spoonful into my mouth before planting a drive-by kiss on my forehead as we head our separate ways.

I dump my backpack in the hall and slip out the side door that leads to the backyard, which is something that people have here in the far eastern reaches of Queens. It's mainly a concrete patch about the size of Mom's Olds, covered by a web of clotheslines. But, if you duck under the soaring sails of old people's undies, the brown bathroom towels with embroidered owls on them, and the nubby pink chenille blankets, you'll find an L-shaped flower bed that wraps around the back perimeter of the yard. The longer side is stocked with Grandma's rosebushes, and the shorter side holds Grandpa's tomato plants.

When Grandpa runs out of wooden dowels to tie his plants to, he commandeers the yardsticks from Grandma's sewing supply closet, but it'll be two decades before I have any idea that it's not totally standard gardening practice to have a bunch of rulers sticking out of your soil. In fact, the first thing I do when I get outside is pluck one of those yardsticks out of the tomato bed and start sprinting from one side of the yard to the other and pole-vaulting myself into the air with it in an attempt to snatch Grandma's wooden clothespins off the line. This would usually be followed later that day by my grandmother chasing me around and around the dining room table with a broken yardstick, screaming, "*Che cazzo!* How many times with the yardsticks!?"

When I've had my fill of yardstick pole-vaulting, I climb over the four-foot chain-link fence that separates Grandma's backyard from Tina and Lenny's, go through their back door without a knock, and weave my way from the kitchen to the living room. The Currancis' house was its own universe of periwinkle and crystal, with the smell of Aqua Net and Chesterfields embedded in the wall-to-wall carpeting. My five-year-old version of an acid trip was to stand dead center in their living room doing pirouettes, with my head tilted completely backward, watching the room whirl by upside-down.

The half-cocked head of Tina, complete with jumbo pink curlers, painted-on eyebrows, and crooked lipstick, pops into my line of vision mid-spin. "Eh! Ya gonna make ya'self sick, you don't stop that!" I snap out of it, "Sorry. Mornin', Tina!" I throw my arms around her waist in a genuinely loving hug but with the less savory secondary intention of sneaking a peek down at her golf-ball-size bunions. *Wow.* And then I'm off.

In three running leaps I cross the concrete driveway that separates Tina and Lenny's house from Anna and Joe's, and land at the Paradises' side door with both my arms straight up over my head like Mary Lou Retton after sticking a floor routine. Their kitchen window is just to the left of the door, and I shout up into it, "I'm heeeeerrrre!!!" In no time, Anna's plump frame appears in the doorway, "G'mornin', my sweetheart!"

She opens the door into her tiny sunlit kitchen full of glowing, '70s-era, harvest-gold appliances. White lace curtains frame the windows, and a ceramic relief of fruit hangs on the wall above the small round oak table—it's about the most pleasant five square feet on Earth. I hop onto a chair at the table and wait for Anna to pour me a glass of orange juice, cut by half with water, as always. We don't say much, but it couldn't be any sweeter. Anna leans into the counter and smiles as I sit there drinking my juice, and when I'm finished, I kiss her on the cheek and skip on out again, this time back to Grandma's house.

If Tina's place is preserved in my memory like some tacky funhouse, and Anna's is a scene from a Norman Rockwell painting, then the two-family house that my grandparents share with Aunt Mary is something of a towering Japanese pagoda. Grandma and Grandpa live on the top tier, Aunt Mary is in the middle, and the bottom level is a finished basement with wall-to-wall folding tables where all thirty members of my immediate family come together for holidays. (In order for us to fit, we kids had to crawl under the first two rows of tables to get to our seats. When someone yelled, "Dinnertime," all eighteen of us would drop onto all fours and make our way through people's legs and around chairs, like a great tide of mice.)

I run back up Grandma's stoop, shoot through the door, up the stairway, and into her kitchen, ready for my debriefing on the day's mission. Let me explain. If other kids spent the odd weekday off from school at Chuck E. Cheese's, say, I might spend mine at Key Foods working up a scheme with my grandmother to get around the ten-per-customer rule on sale items. I can see it now. The two of us are huddled behind a display in the canned-food aisle, and she whispers the plan into my ear: "You take ten, and I take ten. And then you wait on the other line, by yourself, and if the cashier looks at you funny, you say, 'My mother sent me, ALONE, to get these cans of tomatoes.' Then pay and walk out! We'll meet up outside, a few blocks down, on the corner. *Minchia!*"

So I was trained to be ready for anything. But today's particular mission holds great significance for Grandma, which I know, because she had been preparing me for it every day for a week.

"You eat the grapefruit, you leave!" Grandma screams, for no other reason than that's just how she talks. "Mary likes it there alone! It's very nice she invited you for the grapefruit, but that's it! She don't want you to stay long!"

She keeps at me, standing at the stove, her eyes never leaving the pot of tomato sauce she's stirring. "You go downstairs, you eat the grapefruit, you leave!!" After repeating the refrain, for maximum effect, in one fluid motion she rips her wooden spoon up out of the pot, sucks off the sauce, sends it cartwheeling into the sink, and then starts to turn toward me to deliver her typical closer face-to-face, "*Fahng*——" but saves that second syllable until she is fully spun around, "*gool!*" (*Fahngool* is the Italian American pronunciation of the slang word *vaffanculo*, which translates to "go do it in the ass" though is used more like "fuck off." Either way, it's not a nice thing to yell at a five-year-old. But Grandma means nothing by it. "Fuck" is just her go-to, catchall punctuation.)

I'm a few feet below Grandma's sight line, so she's unable to spot me when she first scans the room, her head slowly swiveling left, then right, then left again with a fixed, fuming gaze, looking like a cyborg in a housedress. Right before her eyes start pulsing red and she turns real-life Terminator, her head tilts down, and there I am, standing right at her heels and choking down a laugh because it just occurred to me that, until now, it looked as if she was yelling at her meatballs. But the fun is short-lived. Grandma shoots me a look, and I am right back to being dead serious about my great-aunt Mary's grapefruits.

2

In the three years that I spent among The Geriatrics of 251st Street, I was solidly schooled that the two most important things to Grandma were her older and only sister, Aunt Mary, and her kitchen floor. She referred to the floor only as "my linoleum." If I were to go skipping by on it, she would yell, "Watch with *my linoleum!!*"—the tone of her voice clearly conveying that she was proof positive that her perfectly preserved polyvinyl floor covering would up and crumble beneath the prancing feet of a forty-pound kid. At some point she must have convinced me, because I remember—even if I was running full blast—I would stop dead before I entered the kitchen, then tiptoe over that linoleum like a cartoon cat burglar.

Grandma scrubbed her floor at least three times a day,

jabbing at it rapid-fire with these short, furious strokes that made the mop look like a tommy gun in her hands. And once she was done pumping it full of lead with her mop-*cum*–machine gun, she would get onto her hands and knees to scrub the tough-to-reach edges and corners by hand with a rag.

Of course, before the mopping, and probably an additional half dozen times a day, Grandma first swept the floor, gathering the flecks of dirt, crumbs of Italian bread, and strands of hair into a little pile, as anyone else would do. But then, instead of using a dustpan, she scooped up the pile with the torn halves of an old greeting card. An entire kitchen drawer was dedicated solely to storing all those torn cards, and after Christmas or Easter or her birthday, I helped her replenish the stock. "Come, today you help me rip the cards!" Grandma would say, and I'd follow her around the house, the two of us unsanctimoniously snatching these ill-fated tokens of affection from the windowsills and tabletops. Eventually we'd work our way back to the kitchen table, and, as we sat side by side with little stacks in our laps, she'd take the first card off the top and demonstrate the technique. "Tight, you hold it, like this!" she'd scream, pushing her fisted hand an inch away from my face to make sure I saw the preferred, white-knuckled grip. "Then, high, you lift it, like this!"

Now she'd raise that fist into the air like a Black Power salute. "And with the other hand, you pull down, hard, like THIS"—and *rrrrrip!* "Ah! You see how it tears? Right down the middle! *Minchia!*"

I'd get to work on my stack, looking up at her and dangling my dismembered Hallmark in the air for approval the first few times. She would nod, and soon enough we'd be ripping apart card after card with no more emotion than a pair of farmhands shucking corn. The whole scene strikes me now as some tough-ass urban women's version of elder tribal ladies teaching the wee ones to work a loom: *You see, my dear grandchild, now you're learning the age-old tradition of our people saving two bucks on a dustpan.*

When it came time to scoop up some garbage, and Grandma grabbed a couple of cards from the drawer, perhaps the strangest prayer I ever prayed was that the face-up side, instead of the little cat holding a balloon or some smiling snowman, would be the inside of the card, because I got an extra twinge of irreverent joy watching the inscription—HA*PY B**TH*AY! L*TS OF L*VE, AU*T CAMILLE—disappear under the crumbs.

Right below Grandma's disgraced-greeting-card drawer was a cabinet exploding with dozens of emptied and cleaned plastic Polly-O ricotta containers, Temp Tee cream cheese tubs, and glass Mancini roasted red pepper jars, because Tupperware, like dustpans, was considered an extravagance. So opening Grandma's "Frigidaire" was like peering into a portal to some magical miniature city. And a search for one spoonful of ricotta cheese could turn into a full-on culinary tour of Southern Italy. The last place the cheese would be was in an actual Polly-O container, but you would open it anyway, only to find last night's *braciole*, then to the cream cheese tub stuffed instead with *pasta e fagioli*, and on and on until you were so enticed by everything else, you didn't want ricotta cheese anymore.

On top of these skyscrapers of leftovers, like spires, were dozens of tiny shimmering foil packages. A quarter-inch slice of sausage, a hunk of Parmesan cheese no bigger than a sugar cube, a dollhouse-scale bouquet of cauliflower florets—every last scrap of food was saved, then thrown together come Saturday morning in one of Grandma's off-the-wall-delicious frittatas. Even if I wasn't looking for something to eat, I loved to just stand there and stare.

Anyway, back to my great-aunt and her grapefruits. Having completed her "Don't fuck around at Mary's" speech, Grandma leads me down the single flight of stairs that separates her apartment from her older sister's. At this point, 1985, Grandma is sixty-eight, and Aunt Mary is seventy-two, and in all of their years they have lived either under the same roof or not more than a single city block apart. Their childhood home was a lower-level apartment in a brownstone on Union Street in Park Slope, Brooklyn. After getting married, Aunt Mary moved as far as the upstairs apartment. Grandma made it a hair farther; she got married and moved around the corner. And there the sisters remained until 1978, when they moved to Queens (together, of course).

When we reach the landing, Grandma grabs my hand and shuffles down the hall in her standard-issue, open-toe, terry-cloth slippers, pausing every few steps to look down at me and whisper-scream (all her usual anger, one-eighth her usual volume) her mantra, "You eat the grapefruit, you leave!!" We arrive to find Aunt Mary's door open. Grandma stiff-arms me back as if I'm a lion raring to jump into the crowd, not a stunned five-year-old in the throes of terror because she's about to eat a half a grapefruit with her elderly great-aunt. Grandma juts her head into the doorway and starts screaming again. "Mary! I brought the kid for the grapefruit! You ready? Mary? Mary?! You there!? I got the kid!! Mary? Mary?! You ready!?"

Hours, days, weeks pass before Aunt Mary responds, from somewhere in the abyss, the exaggerated calm of her voice ever so gently reprimanding her sister's craziness. "Y-e-s, Rose. I ... am ... here. I ... am ... ready." Grandma turns back to me, cocks her head, and says, this time only with her eyes, "So, you eat the grapefruit AND ...?" My eyes answer right quick, "I leave!!"

With her palm on the back of my head, Grandma nudges me past the threshold into Aunt Mary's apartment; then she's gone. In front of me is a tiny two-top kitchen table set with two little glasses of water, two serrated grapefruit spoons, two pre-dissected half-grapefruits in flowery china bowls, and, in the center, one of those plastic teddy bears filled with honey. Facing me from across the table is a sweet, smiling wisp of a woman, who, by some miracle, is my grandmother's full-blooded sister.

Compared to my grandma, even a lumberjack could appear frail. With her as my old-lady litmus test, it's entirely possible that Aunt Mary wasn't as much a "wisp" as she was simply "relaxed." But, no matter the exact right way to describe Aunt Mary, it's safe to say that, when contrasted with Grandma, their differences couldn't have seemed more extreme. Grandma bulldozed through a room; Aunt Mary floated. Grandma was squat; Aunt Mary was lithe. Grandma never went more than a minute without cursing, singing, barking orders, or telling raunchy jokes; Aunt Mary was an unofficial mute.

On the whole, Grandma never had much use for dainty

types. When word came over the radio in her kitchen one day that Donna Reed had died, and I asked, "Who's that?" she just replied, "A chump." Sometime later, when I heard the name Mae West and asked Grandma who she was, she said, "My kind of woman, that's who!" In fact, it seemed that Grandma divided all of humankind into these two camps: the Donna Reeds and the Mae Wests. If you were at all "relaxed," like Aunt Mary, or "happy," like my mom, you were instantly deemed a Donna Reed. And Grandma, more Mae West than Mae West, felt herself your personal Catcher in the Rye, taking it as her life's mission to prevent you from falling off that cliff into chump-dom.

Still, Grandma was in awe of Aunt Mary. "A saint, my sister is! And is she elegant? And how!" On the other hand, Grandma was downright petrified that Aunt Mary would come apart at the seams if you as much as sneezed in her direction—which is why she treated my perfectly pleasant, practically wordless, ten-minute, grapefruit-eating date as if it were a private audience with the Pope. Well, that's half the reason.

Several months later, two days after my sixth birthday, I learned the other half. I was out playing in the front yard when I heard the excruciating howls of what I imagined was a dog that had just been hit by a car. I spun around a few times, trying to figure out where the sound was coming from, before my ears pointed me toward Grandma's house. There, crammed into the entryway and spilling out onto the stoop, I made out five of The Geriatrics of 251st Street—Tina, Lenny, Anna, Joe, and Grandpa—and I took off running to reach them.

I jumped and ducked, trying to get a clear view of the source of the strange and awful sound. Finally I dropped to the ground, crawling my way through the crowd, and by the time Anna noticed my head poking out from between her legs, it was too late. Collapsed on the floor of the hallway and wailing in a way that was more animal than human ... was my grandmother. I instantly started crying, too, but kept weaving through the wickets of legs, trying to make my way to her. Before I could reach her, Tina swooped me up into her arms, then shielded my eyes. Both Grandma and I were thrashing and clawing now, me toward her and her toward Aunt Mary's door.

"Mary! Oh, Mary! Oh, my sister!" she cried, as my grandfather hooked his arms under hers and lifted the dead weight of her body up into a folding chair. As soon as he placed her down, Grandma's head fell to her lap with such force that it seemed the momentum might pull the rest of her behind it, so Grandpa quickly dropped to his knees and put his hands on her rounded shoulders to keep her from tumbling to the floor. Grandma stayed that way, head down, back rising and falling with each monstrous sob, as Anna and Tina carried me away.

Family lore has it that, at sixteen, my grandmother cold-cocked a couple of teenage boys for picking on her younger brother Jerry. Then, as a mom, when her middle son—my Uncle Sal—tried to join a Brooklyn gang, she burst into their pool-hall hangout, cursed everybody out, and beat my uncle over the head with her purse until he agreed to come home. Years later, when she was in her late sixties, I watched her chuck a pot of boiling macaroni water at my grandfather because she had convinced herself that he was screwing some lady in New Jersey. The water landed an inch from his feet; hence, she didn't do any time. And, at seventy-five, she won a tug-of-war with a purse-snatcher in an Atlantic City casino by busting the guy's nose open with an elbow to the face, immediately after which she went right back to playing her slot machine. (Mom and I were in the hotel room when she returned, six hours later, and she only mentioned the incident in passing: "The slots are no good to me today, *fahngool* . . . oh, and some guy tried to rob me.") So I am by no means exaggerating when I say that seeing my grandma bawling in a heap on the floor after Aunt Mary died was as devastatingly sad as watching the slow-motion, knee-by-knee collapse of a dying rhino in a *National Geographic* video. Rabid packs of teenage boys, gangs, and thieves posed no threat to her. Like nature's most powerful animals, my grandma had only one true predator: grief.

But, as rocked to the core as I was seeing Grandma in that state the day Aunt Mary died, immediately afterward I was also pretty confused. Up until this time Grandma had handled death with the same awesome irreverence as she did greeting cards. Dying was never referred to as "passing away" or "passing on" or "going to heaven" or pussyfooted around whatsoever; it was only called "croaking." Grandma talked about death as casually as other people talked about last night's ball game. I remember the time I was standing next to her in church when the congregation started the hymn "Here I am, Lord," crooning, "Here I am, Lord. Is it I, Lord? I have heard you calling in the night." She winked at me before she began singing her own doctored lyrics, thrusting her open arms into the air and pointing down at herself, belting, "Here I am, Lord. COME AND GET ME!! I AM READY TO CROAK TONIGHT!!" Afterward, she doubled over laughing so hard at her own joke that her forehead hit the back of the pew in front of us, which only made her laugh harder.

It didn't take long to realize, however, that Aunt Mary's

death was not something we would be joking about. She died in June, and though it was pretty well hidden from me, Mom later said that Grandma spent the entire summer "broken." For reasons we still don't understand, Grandma didn't tell my mother or me until after Aunt Mary died that she had been diagnosed with stage-four lung cancer six months earlier. Suddenly Grandma's ultra-heightened paranoia over my last grapefruit date made sense. But even when it hadn't, I had done as I was told that day: I ate the grapefruit, and I left.

The sole upside to Aunt Mary's death is that it was the catalyst that took me from having a VIP guest pass to the wonderful world of The Geriatrics of 251st Street to being a full-fledged member. Not long afterward it was decided that Mom and I would take over Aunt Mary's apartment.

There was little to deliberate over. My grandparents couldn't afford the house on their own, and my grandmother had never lived with anyone who wasn't blood. Since Grandma took care of me after school, I was already going to PS 133 in Bellerose, as opposed to a school in Rosedale, where I technically lived, so living there would mean a lot less shuttling around for Mom.

So it was that, at age six, I single-handedly brought

the average age of The Geriatrics of 251st Street down from seventy-three to sixty-four. That was much more of a jump for me than them, and it soon took its toll on all my senses. By the start of first grade, my normal speaking voice was a good ten times louder than anyone else under seventy-five. My music was Cab Calloway, Ella Fitzgerald, Frank Sinatra, and not much else. I had developed a serious affinity for sugar-free sucking candy, butterscotch, and Chuckles. Truth is, I absolutely hated Chuckles, but I ate them by the fistful anyway, solely to spite Grandma. If moving in had brought me any new insights, it was that the third most important thing to her, beyond Aunt Mary and her linoleum, was proving to the world that we were not starving. Like most people who'd endured the Depression, Grandma was obsessed with food. Unlike sane people, however, she remained so obsessed that even by the mid 1980s she still needed to let our neighbors know that we had enough to eat.

One way this insanity manifested itself was that she was constantly trying to feed us. For example, if I was playing outside but had to come in to use the bathroom, even if it was 11:00 a.m., she refused to let me go back outside until I had downed a plate of macaroni. (I went to great lengths to get around this—once, just once, by shitting in a bucket in her garden.)

And the other way was that she forbade me from eating anyone else's food. For her, a neighbor's seemingly innocuous heaping candy dish was, in reality, a booby trap, meant to reveal whether I was malnourished. Or, if I were to take a piece of candy, she thought someone would instantly assume, "Poor kid must be starving. She ate a Chuckle."

Each week she gave me the same speech. "We're going for cards tonight at Tina's. Now, if she says to you, 'Here, have a candy,' you say, 'No, I'm full, thank you.' You eat! We don't want them to think you don't eat over here! *Fahngool!*" Everyone thought she was nuts, but nobody was going to square off with her. Instead, they found a simpler solution: Tina would give me an extra deck of cards and tell me to crawl under the table to play. Then Tina, Lenny, my grandfather, Anna, and Joe would sneak handfuls of Chuckles down to me. Eventually the candies would be coming in from all angles, more hands than there should have been for that number of people, it seemed. They tasted awful, especially with four or five jammed in my mouth at once. But that never stopped me from finishing every single one.

Living on 251st Street full-time also brought the opportunity for me to make friends with the handful of kids on the block. Although, my version of friendship at the time was to show up and anoint myself Mob Boss. I led a crew that included a little Polish girl named Kristin Petekie-wicz, whose name Grandma always forgot, so she referred to her instead as "the quiet one with the snot," and who I truly loved but still bossed around and once convinced to eat a handful of grass. Then there was Dennis, a scrawny German boy who I talked into the "you show me yours, I'll show you mine" bit behind his garage after school one day. And Peter, a Puerto Rican kid who I made my lackey in one of my more unsavory plots that year, when an In-dian boy our age moved onto the block. I got five-year-old Peter to ring his doorbell while I hid behind a nearby bush. When the kid answered, I told Peter to say, "Tara Clancy has unfinished business with you!" Right after which I jumped out, flying-squirrel style, and pounced on him—all because somebody told me he had six toes on his right foot.

I wasn't half as tough as I thought I was, because when he started to cry, I burst into tears, too. I even blubbered out a whole string of "I'm sorry"s as he ran back into the house, but it was too late. A second later his mother came out, pure rage in a deep red sari, and in no time flat Grandma was there too, staring down at me and rattling the wad of keys in the front pocket of her housedress the same way a cowboy spins his pistol before the shoot-out. She shook her head at me without a word for a long while before finally looking up and saying to the lady, "I'm very sorry, ah . . . this one is just a little nuts sometimes!" His mother nodded and then, to our surprise, invited us in. It was a lovely gesture, but nobody knew what to do or say next. The four of us stood silently in her kitchen, a whole heap of pots clanking away on the stove and ratcheting up the tension, until Grandma finally said, "So, you cook, ah?" His mother said yes, Grandma said, "Me, too," they both smiled, and that was enough for a truce on 251st Street.

A few days later I rang the boy's bell to see if he wanted to come out to play, and he did, but not before we cleared things up. Through his screen door he said, "Just so you know, my mother says that having six toes is good luck." And I said, believing this to be gospel, "Wow. I had no idea!" The rest of the crew was waiting on the sidewalk, and as we walked out to join them, I said, "So, hey, I got this idea for us all to make some money today. You want in?" He did.

I led everybody to Grandma's backyard, where I had laid out sheets of construction paper on the ground alongside a little pile of crayons. We all huddled together, and I lifted up a sample sheet, which I had already prepared, a bright pink piece of paper with two blue squiggly lines. "This," I announced, "is called 'abstract art,' and if we all make a few of these, we can go around the neighborhood selling them for a buck apiece! C'mon, take a crayon!"

When my mom got home from work that night, she found me counting out a stack of dollar bills in my room, and she flipped out. "Tara! Honey, people bought those drawings from you because you're a kid and they thought it was cute. But you can't do that; it's not right. What did you say to these people?"

"I said that in the city there's a place called Sotheby's where people sell drawings like these for a lot of money, but you can get this one for just a dollar!"

And the reason I knew that to be true? Well, that brings us back to the limo ride.

3

I'm the lone fish in a forty-foot tank, an ant in an airplane hangar, that last guy sitting in the stands of an emptied arena—I am a seven-year-old girl in a sleeveless Bruce Springsteen concert T-shirt, cutoff jean shorts, and beat-up Nike high-tops, sitting in the back of a stretch limousine, lumbering out of the farthest-flung corner of Queens.

The dark-tinted windows have turned day to night in an instant, a phenomenon that I understand at seven but that scared the ever-living shit out of me the very first time I rode alone in one of these things. I was only five then, and, unfamiliar with the wonders of window tinting, I could not fathom how the summer-morning sky had gone black the very second I stepped into the car. I panicked, figuring that the End of Days I'd been hearing about at CCD (Sunday school) was upon us, until it finally occurred to me to try opening the damn window. And in a flash I went from petrified to ecstatic. Window closed: Apocalypse. Window open: bright summer day! Closed: Doomsday. Open: sunshine!! I must have worn the button down to a nub that day—two years later, I still need to check, but I'm satisfied after just a few rounds.

As a matter of principle I keep staring out the window until my exit from Broad Channel is official, which is when we've passed the great wall of Call-A-Head blue plastic Porta Potties. I watch as, one by one, they slide out of view, the long row magically shrinking down to nothing, and only then do I turn back in. I take a breath—the infamous rotten-egg/septic-tank Broad Channel air has been replaced with the newly vacuumed limo air, mixed with Windex and the driver's aftershave. My nose twitches as I try to figure if I like one better than the other. I don't.

I take a long look around the inside of the car and let the emotional pendulum swing: *I'm such a small kid in this big car, alone, it's scary . . . I'm such a small kid in this big car, alone . . . I can do whatever I want!* The pendulum goes back and forth a few more times before I remember how to balance it out.

Popping open the seat belt that only two minutes ago I promised my dad I'd keep on for the whole ride, I unpeel the sweat-glued bare skin on my thighs from the leather upholstery and slide across the bench seat until I'm sitting at the very center with my feet propped on the carpeted hump in the floor. Then, in a further attempt to spread myself out and make the space feel a bit smaller, I chest-pass my overnight bag all the way across the car to the bench seat opposite me. The bag is a nylon, '80s-variety gym duffel, and looking at it lying there all small and limp has the opposite effect, but it feels good to be flinging shit around anyway.

Directly above me is the most wonderful one square foot of plastic I know to exist, ten times better than any toy, and I spend a few seconds just staring up, mouth agape, drinking it in. It is the Overhead Control Panel, a hundred thousand (really just ten or so) buttons, switches, and dials, and I must, MUST, press, turn, or flip each and every one, every time I make this trip. (I have only one memory of a driver complaining that I turned the first twenty minutes of the ride into something like the sound-and-light check for a KISS show at the Garden. He yelled, "Eh, kid! I think it's time to quit it with all that! . . . Eh! Kid? . . . Eh, you!?" I snapped out of my obsessive button-pushing eventually but only long enough to say, "Sorry, mister, I just got a few more to go!")

I hop up onto my knees (I'm too short to reach the

panel from my seat) and dive in. Partition all the way up, then all the way down, and repeat. Moonroof open, shut, repeat, repeat, repeat. I hit every preset button on the radio, fiddle with the tuner dial for a good five minutes, blast the volume when "Pour Some Sugar on Me" comes on, then lower it back down, mid fist pump, when I get a glare from the driver in the rearview.

I turn on and off all the interior mood lighting, switch the fan speed from light breeze to gale-force wind, and twist the temperature control knob from Arctic to Boca and back. I eye the intercom buttons last but hesitate for a little bit before finally working up the nerve to press LISTEN. I eavesdrop for five nerve-racking seconds' worth of static backed by the hum of tires on asphalt, then damn near fall over when the driver clears his throat. In my mind, this is the crime of the century.

With my heart beating at hummingbird rate, I plop back down onto the seat. And if in this moment I wasn't some kid in a limo, but an actor on TV playing the office underling who just stole a minute in his boss's desk chair after he'd gone home for the day, this would be when I would lean back, crack my knuckles, and start rubbing my palms together. *Now, let's see what's in these drawers!*

I stand up (I'm so short, I can do that even though I'm inside a car) and beeline it for the black-lacquered shelving unit. On top is a refrigerator-egg-holder-style cutout caddy holding a half dozen highball glasses, and I spin them in place, one by one. Working my way right, I pull the square crystal stopper from the first of the three spirit-filled decanters, then, knowing the shock to my nasal passages that is to come, I ever so slowly extend my nose over the top to take a whiff. *Woo!* I get that cockeyed-wince face and pull my head away ... but when my eyelids stop fluttering and my nose stops burning, I do the exact same thing with the next decanter in line: *Damn!!* And the next: *Aw, man!!!*

Below the row of glasses and bottles of booze are several closed compartments. Per usual, I'm as excited to discover what's inside as I am by their ultra luxurious push-to-open latches. Cabinets without handles: *Wow!* First I use a slight, two-finger touch. I'm blown away by the slow, grand way the door unhinges. But before I even bother looking inside, I shut it again and try a few other variations: superfast single-finger poke, karate-style palm strike—*Hi-ya!*, etc.

Inside the first compartment is a tiny television, and as soon as I see it, I start praying to the gods of Hanna-Barbera. I flip the stations in a frenzy for a good five minutes, but I don't find a single Smurf, Jetson, or Flintstone, so I move along. Another cabinet contains an ice bin stocked with half-pint glass soda bottles, and though experience has taught me that these only ever offer club soda or tonic, I take them all out, hoping I'll find a Veryfine fruit punch or a quarter water* anyway.

Having had my fill of the shelving unit, I dive onto the back-facing bench seat nearest the partition. I lie there with my hands under my head and my elbows butterflied out and stare at the ceiling for a bit, until inspiration hits: I sit up, run across the floor, and dive onto the bench on the other side. I dart back and forth now, flinging myself sidelong into the seats and springing back up into the air like a WWF wrestler bouncing off the ropes. I somersault off the seat, play pin Hulk Hogan, then start pounding the floor, "Ladies and gentlemen, it looks as if the Hulk is down for the count! One, two, three, fo— no, wait, he's up! He's up!!" Now I'm doing elbow drops and clotheslines. I imagine myself in a kilt and a "Hot Rod" T-shirt—I'm "Rowdy" Roddy Piper! I cross my eyes and curl my lip—I'm "Hacksaw" Jim Duggan! I flex my biceps—I'm "Macho Man" Randy Savage! I collapse

* "Quarter waters" are what city kids called a sugary, Kool-Aid–like drink sold in tiny plastic barrels with a foil top. They could be found on the very bottom shelf, or just the floor, of any deli refrigerator in Queens and were the cheapest drink option. I don't think they're around anymore—I guess they just didn't sell once the price went up. "Fifty-cent waters" doesn't have the same ring.

onto the seat, covered in sweat, out of breath, and damn pleased with myself. "Winner and undisputed champion of the world, "Scooter" "Shrimpy" "Chickenella" Tara Clancy!!" (Mom gave me that last nickname, an English/Italian mash-up that she ascribed to me at birth because I had short, scrawny, "chicken" legs.)

By the time I'm done with all my button-pushing, liquor-sniffing, cabinet-opening, channel-switching, and WrestleMania-making, a good hour has gone by, and we are now a long way from the boat sheds and bungalows of Broad Channel, Queens. I look out the window to find the familiar, never-ending row of evergreens lining the Long Island Expressway and decide to kill a little more time with another one of my favorite games. I pick a tree in the distance to focus on and follow it with my eyes as we approach, my neck turning slowly at first and then snapping to the right just before it disappears from view. Then I zing my head all the way back to the left, like a typewriter jumping to a new line, choose another tree, and start over. I can keep this up for at least ten minutes.

The very last part of my limo-riding routine was to pop my head through the partition and chitchat with the driver. And I always opened with the same line: "So, you got any kids?" On this day, like most others, I get a big smile followed by a finger pointing to a couple of dog-eared, wallet-size school photos tucked into a lip on the dash. That's all I need; I'm off to the races, motor-mouthing for the next five minutes, asking question after question but never giving the poor guy enough time to actually answer them. "What school do your kids go to? I go to PS 133. I have Mrs. Stulberg, she's a'right. I like sports better than school, though. Your kids play sports? I'm the fastest kid in my whole grade, faster than the boys and everything, really! My favorite team is the Mets. You a Mets fan? You ever see a game at Shea? My dad took me once. My favorite players are Gary Carter and Darryl Strawberry, I got their Starting Lineup figures, too. Who's your favorite player?"

Whether an actual conversation started to happen or I just finally ran out of things to say and we went silent, for the last half hour of the trip I always stayed in this position, kneeling on the seat, head poking through the partition, anxiously scanning left and right, ticking off my mental checklist of landmarks: *The Lobster Inn, the windmill, that farm stand with the pies, Main Street! Caldor, IGA, Penny Whistle Toys, Bobby Van's, J.G. Melon's, Ocean Road! The golf course, that gigantic house on the left, Jobs Lane! First potato field, cornfield, Colin Powell's house* (whoever that is), *second potato field . . . slow crunch of gravel under the tires, driveway!*

And, some two hours after Tommy O'Reilly knocked

my lights out in front of the converted boat-shed trailer of a house I lived in with my dad every other weekend or whatever odd holidays and random weeknights when I wasn't with The Geriatrics of 251st Street, I had arrived in Bridgehampton, one of the handful of seaside towns collectively known as the Hamptons, the summertime getaway of New York City's rich and famous . . . and, for the last five years, a sunshiney Brooklyn-Italian social worker–*cum*–cleaning lady/waitress who was just then hauling ass toward the limo parked in the driveway of her boyfriend's estate, screaming, "My Chickenellahh!!!"

4

My mother was always out of place, even when she wasn't. As a kid she preferred the Brooklyn Botanic Garden or the library to the ball games and beauty parlors where other girls with names like Carmella Riccobono hung out. And when all her friends were squirreling away their allowances and birthday money for records and roller skates, she was saving hers for a porcelain vase she had spotted at her uncle Jerry's antiques shop in upstate New York.

Going from Park Slope, Brooklyn, to Uncle Jerry's home in Pleasant Valley every summer was the only family vacation my mother and her five siblings had ever had, and my grandmother squeezed as much mileage from it as she could: *Madonna! If you don't stop with the noise, nobody is going to Jerry's! You had better finish that good food I made you, or nobody is going to Jerry's! You don't want to listen? Nobody is going to Jerry's!*

My grandmother's incessant threats, though brilliant at invoking both fear and guilt, were nonetheless empty—they *always* made it to "Uncle Jelly's." My mom and her siblings gave him this nickname not because they couldn't pronounce *Jerry*, but because it suited him. His un-Americanized name was Giulio, which, like Jelly, was a lot more appropriate for a man who was forever in an ascot and captain's hat, collected nineteenth-century birdcages, and whose life partner, John, was an interior decorator.

They had met at my great-grandfather's restaurant, where Uncle Jerry, along with all four of his brothers, worked as waiters. It was family-style Italian trattoria on the second floor of a factory building on West 37th Street in Manhattan's garment district, with checkered tablecloths, finger-loop gallon jugs of wine served by the glass, and no menus—the brothers announced the day's specials. "Today we have chicken or porgies. What'll it be?" The joint was as simple as simple could be, but it was nonetheless called the El Dorado.

(I have always admired the overwhelming optimism of immigrants who name their humble restaurants after grand wonders, like the greasy Chinese takeout joint called The Great Wall of China, or the bare-fluorescent-tube-lit

Indian place with tablecloth-less, church-basement-style card tables called Taj Mahal 2. And I feel a strange pride that my great-grandfather did the same thing, maybe even more so for his choosing the mythical South American city of gold over something actually Italian.)

After a few years together Uncle Jerry left the restaurant to work with John in the decorating business, and they bought a home upstate.

A sprawling country house on a lake with a screened-in flagstone porch, library, fully appointed Victorian-era dining room, and a half dozen bedrooms meticulously decorated with antique furniture, Oriental rugs, and lush silk curtains, Uncle Jerry's home was my mother's very own Versailles. Back in Brooklyn, Mom shared a twin bed with her youngest sister, Lucille, in their parents' bedroom. And, though a three-bedroom apartment housing a family of eight was not exceptionally small by Brooklyn standards, Uncle Jerry's space was a complete revelation for her.

While Mom's brothers and sister did a perfunctory spin around the house before darting outside to play in the grass and trees, she would slowly work her way through each room, running her fingers across the mahogany dressers and night tables, ogling the candelabra and porcelain statues. Midafternoon, when Uncle Jerry would announce that he was heading over to his little antiques shop nearby, she was the only one interested in tagging along.

It was on one of these trips that she first spotted the vase. She was only eleven years old, helping her uncle tidy up, when it peeked out from behind her feather duster. She stopped, straining her neck to follow the winding pattern of birds and flowers around the back, afraid to actually touch the vase to turn it around. Eventually she stepped back to gain perspective, time flying by as she fantasized about where it might have come from, how many homes it had been in, and what the types of people who'd owned such a delicate and beautiful thing might have looked like.

The vase's $75 price tag was one hell of a sum in 1963. And my grandmother just could not understand. "*Minchia!* What a little girl wants with such a thing, I'll never know?!" But my mother was undeterred. And, after combining all the allowance money she had saved for years, and pleading on her birthday and Christmas that, instead of toys and dresses, her parents, grandparents, and multitudes of aunts and uncles consider contributing toward her vase fund, when she was twelve years old, it became hers. Since then, the vase has gone wherever my mother has. That is, for over fifty years *she* has been the type of person who owns such a delicate and beautiful thing; hers are the homes in which it has lived.

By Mom's teenage years, as most of her friends hardened into rough-around-the-edges Brooklyn types, she bloomed into a flower child, at least in her head. God knows, she wasn't allowed to act on that. My grandmother practiced a mighty brand of "smother love"—born only to Depression-era, street-fighting, crucifix-swinging Catholics, the defining characteristic of whom was a perpetual sense of impending doom that extended from this world to the next. So maybe my mom hummed "Age of Aquarius" to herself before going to bed, but that was it; no way was my grandmother letting her buy those "wackadoo" records. For my mother, even being allowed to join friends for a trip to Coney Island or the movies was a real rarity, and sleeping over at a friend's house was completely forbidden. In fact, having friends at all was something my grandmother questioned, "What, you don't have enough cousins!?"

My mother was desperate to go to college, not least because it meant getting out from under my grandmother's constant eye. But Grandma hadn't finished high school, and, though all of my mother's five siblings had, none of them went to college. So, again, just like wanting the vase, or friends, my mother's interest in continuing her education was something my grandmother just could not understand, "What for? You're gonna get married, no!?" Still,

Mom begged and begged, and when that didn't work, she offered to split the tuition.

Starting in high school and throughout college my mother worked the concession stands at Yankee and Shea stadiums on the weekends with her dad. And at seventeen she also took on a weeknight job manually stamping routing numbers on checks in a production line of teenage girls in the basement of the Chase Bank offices at One Penn Plaza in Manhattan.

All in all, with the money from both jobs, Mom had enough to pull off half the tuition at St. Joseph's College. That the school was Catholic and in Brooklyn were the only reasons my grandmother allowed her to "throw her money away," adding, *"Stunad!"* (stupid idiot) and slowly shaking her head before giving her daughter a short, slight smile and agreeing to kick in the other half. There is still a whole lot of love in smother love.

Sitting on a canvas-wrapped stack of newly laundered tablecloths locked inside the unlit cargo compartment of a tinny box truck, my mother was pretty damn literally delivered to her fate.

She was eighteen, a freshman at St. Joseph's and still living at home in Brooklyn, when she was invited to a party in Rockaway, Queens. Neither she nor my grandmother had a driver's license, never mind a car, but my grandfather had the truck he drove for Linens of the Week. If it was a special occasion, and a weekend, he was more than happy to offer his kids a lift—throughout high school my mother and her girlfriends had ridden to all their school dances in the back of that truck, teetering atop bags of clean, folded napkins, aprons, and dishrags.

So, in the summer of 1970, having accepted a new college friend's invitation to a party, and after what was likely my mom's very last ride in the back of my grandfather's linens truck, she slipped off her stack of tablecloths, hurried down 108th Street in Rockaway, and headed into McNulty's Bar and Dance Club, where she'd meet a guy from the next town over, Broad Channel.

Carmella Ann Riccobono met Gilbert Francis Anthony Clancy Junior at the bar in McNulty's, and they quickly took to the dance floor. As she describes him, "He had that 'Irish look,' which I liked—the opposite of me, I guess—sparkly blue eyes, light brown hair. He was very cute, really, but short. What is he, five-eight, your father? So what?! He could dance!"

"Yeah, I danced," my dad has admitted. "You got girls if you danced, so I did. Was pretty good, too!"

My father was twenty to her eighteen. Her father was a truck driver; his had been a sign painter. She had five siblings; he had six: Gilbert, Arthur, Margaret, Dennis, Gilbert again (my dad, and, nope, we have no idea why either), Thomas, and Michael.

Like my mother, he wanted to go to college, but while my mom's family was working class, my dad's was poor. Neither of his parents had finished high school, nor did most of his siblings, and though he graduated with honors, he knew his family needed him to kick in as soon as possible. Five years before my parents met, when Dad was fifteen, his father had to stop working. My grandfather had been so severely burned by mustard gas back in the war that, all those years later, his left leg had to be amputated and replaced with a wooden prosthetic. The whole thing would have been incredibly tragic save for the fact that my father entertained the family by throwing darts at it. Even my grandfather got a kick out of it . . . until the one day my dad missed and got him in the real leg.

"Nobody had money back then" is Dad's response to how having to go to work straight out of high school to support his family made him feel. "The guy who owned Johnson's—you know, the bar—his kid always had the stuff he wanted, Lionel trains 'n' all that, and, yeah, I loved trains, so I was jealous of that, but other kids growing up in Broad Channel didn't have three meals a day—the Spencers, phew! Nuns at St. Virgilius used to put the leftover rice pudding from lunch aside for them kids to bring home as dinner! You wanna talk about college?! Look, Scooter, we didn't have it that bad, but we didn't have money either."

By the time he met my mom, Dad had already put in two years as a trainee at the 101st police precinct in Far Rockaway. You couldn't go into the police academy until you were twenty-one, but trainees were paid a minimal salary to do clerical work in the station, and my dad was so underweight that one of his superiors told him he needed to use the three years to bulk up anyway. His boss insisted he eat a pound of bananas a day, which my dad did for so many days that at some point, and forever after, his face started contorting at the mere sight of one.

At nineteen, after my parents had been dating for a year, my mother tried to move out of her parents' house to be on her own. Her plan was to live with her friend Barbara

"Rollie" Iorollo and experience a little independence before deciding whether or not to marry my dad. But, knowing that my grandmother wouldn't go for that plan, she plotted a quick escape.

Rollie pulled up outside my grandparents' brownstone one night, engine running, and my mom, suitcase in hand, walked up to my grandmother in the living room and blurted out the lines she had been rehearsing for an hour: "Ma, my friend is here to pick me up, and I'm leaving. I'm going to move in with her, and—"

But before my mom could finish, my grandmother started wheezing. As my mom remembers it, Grandma went from zero to sixty in a flash—her chest started heaving, little beads of sweat rolled down the sides of her face, her inhalations growing longer and louder by the second, until, suddenly, with a great slap to the heart, she collapsed into a chair. My mother dropped her luggage and ran to her side.

"I'll DIE! I'll die if you leave!!" Grandma screamed. My mother fell to the floor, wrapped her arms around my grandmother's legs, and sobbed, "I won't go, Ma. Please! Please calm down! I'll stay, I promise." To this day, my mother isn't sure if my grandmother faked it. But that near heart attack, feigned or not, may be the reason I am here.

5

On Sunday, July 22, 1973, my mom walked down the aisle at St. Francis Xavier Church in Park Slope, Brooklyn, to meet my father at the altar. My parents' reason for dating hadn't boiled down to much more than a mutual physical attraction paired with a mutual "This is just what ya do" philosophy. So there they were, getting married in a ceremony officiated by not one but two priests—Father Petrowski and Father Maloney, the former of her home parish and the latter of my father's St. Virgilius in Broad Channel.

At the wedding reception, per Italian tradition, my parents went from table to table with a cream-colored satin string-tie satchel collecting *abusta*, envelopes filled with money.

And then, per Irish tradition and to my mother's dismay, everyone on my father's side, from the geriatric great-aunts to the pimply-faced teenage nephews, got good and drunk. In defense of my Irish family, and according to my mother, only a small handful of them truly went overboard. And, if Italian tradition had not been to lock up their daughters so tightly (even that night at McNulty's my grandfather waited outside in his truck for my mom, and afterward, on all of my parents' dates before the wedding, she was always to be home by 9:00 p.m.), she may well have seen this coming, and either not have been so shocked or at least known when it was in good fun or not. (Unfortunately, as the subsequent years progressed, with the murder rate in his precinct climbing and the day-to-day violence my father saw on the job taking its toll on him, my mother would learn the difference between "good, fun drinking" and the other kind.)

Following the wedding my parents lived in an apartment in Windsor Terrace, Brooklyn, one neighborhood over from where Mom had grown up. But after a year they moved to a house in Rosedale, Queens—which my mother then called "the country." Dad considers their having bought a house together the reason it "wasn't all bad, you see? That's something!" For my mom's part, the plus side was: "Well, he taught me to drive! He let me use his green Dodge Dart—paid for lessons and everything."

Neither of my parents has offered me much in the way of romantic stories from their time together following that fateful night at McNulty's Bar and Dance Club. What they have given me is some idea of what their lives looked like in the few years before I was born, which helped me understand why those romantic stories were missing in the first place.

My father was then assigned to the 75th precinct in Bedford-Stuyvesant, Brooklyn—which at the time had the highest homicide rate in the city's history. My mother spent a long while trying to convince him to find another type of work. "I was scared shit," she told me, "but your father sincerely wanted to help people, and he thought this was the way to do that. I loved him for it, but I didn't think it would pan out that way. He didn't listen to me— didn't complain either, though. He didn't talk about it at all, as a matter of fact. But it wouldn't be long before I could see that the job was changing him."

Having earned her degree in social work from St. Joseph's, Mom was hired as a caseworker for Catholic Charities. It was 1974, and she was assigned to split her time between their Bushwick, Brooklyn, and Far Rockaway, Queens, offices, two of the roughest neighborhoods in New York City at the time. In the former, she worked mostly with teenage girls fleeing gangs. For a long while she felt she was in over her head, but she liked to listen, and the girls trusted her enough to talk. As she puts it, "Hard as they had it, those girls had hope, and I saw them progress."

It was a very different story at her Queens assignment. In Far Rockaway my mother split her time between counseling alcohol- and drug-addicted teens at a clinic and tracking down families who had abandoned their terminally ill children at a local hospital (unfortunately, this is something of a known phenomenon). One of the teens she counseled was a poor Irish addict named Teresa, whom my mother grew particularly close with. After a year of consistently making her regularly scheduled appointments, one day Teresa was late. Finally my mom went out into the neighborhood looking for her. She found her, not far from the clinic, dead in the street from an overdose. Just a short time later, after my mom had successfully counseled a woman who had stopped visiting her ill child to return to the hospital, the child died an hour before the mother arrived. "It was like some terrible, terrible movie," she remembers.

After six years, she was coming home from her job as dejected and depressed as my father did from his. And when she became pregnant with me, she knew that, once I was born, she would have to take a break from her job.

My mom stayed home with me until my first birthday.

My parents were barely able to pay their bills on my dad's NYPD salary alone, and she had reached a point where she was looking under the couch cushions for change to buy me milk every week. So when a friend mentioned that her boss was looking for someone to clean his apartment, Mom decided to take the job. "No drug overdoses, no dying children, and—sad as it was—better pay."

The boss's apartment was in a neighborhood about fifteen miles from where we then lived in Rosedale, Queens, less than ten from where my mom had grown up in Brooklyn, less than five from where she'd once worked, in the city, and yet she had never even heard of this part of town before. "A lot of people haven't heard of it. Don't worry, it's *technically* part of Manhattan," her friend reassured her.

After rattling and scraping her way down a dingy side street somewhere in Long Island City, Queens, my mother arrived at the base of an ominous, rusted-metal drawbridge that looked like it belonged in some Pennsylvania steel-mill town, not New York City. At the sight of it she threw the car into park, and, for what felt like the tenth time since she'd left our house twenty minutes earlier, she once again combed over the directions. And, once again, she was shocked to find that she was still on course.

Go over weird little bridge.

The bridge crossed a tiny expanse of water nowhere near wide enough to be the East River, and it delivered her not onto a Manhattan street, but directly into a six-story, monolithic parking garage with the word MOTORGATE in Helvetica painted vertically down a concrete beam.

Mom spiraled her way up the garage ramp until she finally found an empty slot. *Take elevator to street. Take red bus. Get off at 505 Main St.* The "red bus" part grabbed her attention—all other city buses at the time were blue or green. And as soon as the elevator doors opened at street level, idling right outside was a red bus with the words RED BUS printed along its side.

After watching everyone in front of her board the red bus without paying, when it was her turn to step inside, Mom started to go for her change purse anyway. "It's okay, miss," the driver said, "it really is free." Now she was warier than ever—the only free bus rides in New York City she'd ever heard of were the ones that took you to the psych ward or prison.

From what she could see, Main Street was the only street on this peculiar little island, and it had just one lane going in each direction, with red buses going to and fro and hardly any other cars on the road. Lining both sides of the street were hulking buildings with all the charm of those prefab concrete jobs favored in Eastern Bloc countries, and on their ground levels, a handful of small dim shops with generic, uniform signage: DRY CLEANER, DELI, RESTAURANT. *Manhattan, my ass,* my mother thought. *This is the strangest and ugliest place I have ever seen.*

Once again she checked her directions—this time to be sure she hadn't missed the part about a portal transporting her to some dystopian future.

It wasn't until she was standing right in front of 505 Main Street that Mom was finally sure she wasn't in the year 2075, or 1960s Czechoslovakia, and that her friend's description of her boss as a "well-off businessman" made sense. With the prerequisite backward head tilt she surveyed this brand-new twenty-story beast of a building, then stutter-stepped a few times in front of the revolving doors, like a kid getting ready to jump into a game of double Dutch, before figuring out how and when to hop in. With a rush of air and a glint of light, she was suddenly inside a cavernous lobby that smelled appropriately of floor polish and air freshener but with a puzzling hint of chlorine. To her right, sitting at a chest-high, half-moon reception desk was a doorman in full uniform and cap. To her left was a long row of glass windows behind which was the source of the mysterious chlorinated air: an Olympic-size indoor pool. *Wow,* she couldn't help thinking, *so this is how people with money live.*

Though my mother didn't know it at the time—and it's probably a good thing that she didn't—only ten years earlier this neighborhood was still officially named Welfare Island. For over a hundred years it was best known for having almshouses for the city's poor, a smallpox hospital, a place called the New York City Lunatic Asylum, and a penitentiary where Billie Holiday and Mae West (my grandmother's hero) once served time. In 1971, after nearly all these institutions had shuttered their doors and the island was largely abandoned, a complete redevelopment effort was set into motion. The construction of several residential complexes began, including a few luxury high-rises—505 Main Street was among the very first—and Welfare Island was renamed Roosevelt Island (with the wonderfully self-effacing tagline, "Manhattan's *other* island").

And it is in this very place that my mother's journey from being a cleaning lady to the type of person who "summered in the Hamptons" began.

In the end, my mother cleaned the businessman's apartment for a full year before they actually met, but she says she knew the very minute she first walked into his place that she would like him. For a person whose prized possession at the age of twelve was an antique vase, it might come as no surprise that it wasn't the *size* of his place that most impressed her (though her friend forgot to tell her it was a duplex) or even the panoramic view of the Manhattan skyline (though she spent nearly a half hour at the end of the job staring out the window), but his antique furniture and artwork.

She had presumed that a single, well-off man's apartment would be some terrible display of wealth and nothing more—a smattering of the tacky 1980s furniture she despised, purchased by an assistant or some hip minimalist decorator, maybe. Instead, she opened the door, and her feet stayed glued to the floor; it was as if she was right back at Uncle Jelly's home (only better, and minus the antique mahogany birdcage collection, making it slightly more possible that this businessman was not gay).

The floors were covered in antique Persian rugs, and the walls were lined with gold-framed paintings and brass candle sconces. The rustic round farmhouse table in the dining room was fully set with white linen napkins, real silverware, and fine porcelain plates, and behind it was a matching pine hutch that held floral-painted soup tureens, pitchers, and bowls. In the living room were tufted wingback chairs with claw feet, a brass-tacked olive-green leather couch with a worn steamer trunk for a coffee table, and a highly polished, ornate wooden inlaid desk. All the pieces were from completely different eras, but they worked together—she could tell right away how carefully chosen, looked after, and loved they were. She was blown away.

One day my mom arrived to her cleaning job to find a note on the kitchen counter next to a heap of dirty pots and pans in the sink:

So sorry for the extra dishes. I have been taking an Indian cooking class and experimenting like mad! —Mark

My god, she thought, *an Indian cooking class? Who* is *this guy?* He was a complete departure from any man she'd ever known.

As Mom was cleaning Mark's apartment, I was making a mess of ours. One day I toddled up to the end table that held my mother's treasured vase and took a swat at it. From as early as I can remember straight up to today, my father has told and retold the story of what came next between his baby girl and his wife's beloved antique vase with the same long-drawn-out sense of drama he otherwise reserves for retellings of horse races, ball games, and bar fights. And like any storytelling dad worth his salt, the tale always starts the same way: "I ever tell you 'bout the time . . . ?"

"Yup, you have. But tell it again, Da!" He shakes his head no, feigning that he isn't going to go on, and I urge, "C'mon! What's the story?"

"What? What!? You damn near got us killed, is what!! Musta turned away no more than a second, and by the time I turn back, there you are, all shit-eating grin, just about to take a swing. Your mother's most prized possession! And I think, oh, boy, this is it—Mel's gonna kill us both! Now, as luck would have it, you couldn't reach it, short little shit that you were, but you musta clipped the table edge, and that thing just took off, straight up into the air! Higher and higher it went, till it just stopped, as if the little bastard was giving me a wink before, of course, down it came! Now, I'm on the couch, right? And I figure I got one shot here, so I make like I'm stealing second base, stretching my leg out and under it, and—I shit you not—that vase hit my thigh, lengthwise, and started to roll, straight down, over my knee, down my shin, all the way to my toes and right onto the floor, without as much as a chip. Scooter, it was a miracle if I ever saw one!"

As my parents tell it, the vase incident was a poor primer for the havoc-wreaking tear I would go on in the final months of their relationship. There was the time, just after my second birthday, when I crept up to the cooler my dad kept next to his recliner on game days, stole one of his Budweiser nips, and ran off to hide. Some thirty minutes of fruitless searching had passed before my poor mother collapsed in the bathroom, sitting on top of the toilet, sobbing into her hands as she contemplated calling the cops about her missing daughter. Only then did she hear the giggling and found me, a few feet away, hiding in the shower stall with a bit of a buzz on, holding a half-drunk Bud.

Next up was the time my father decided to relax by sprawling out on the hardwood floor of our living room with a pillow under his head, and I ran up behind him and purposefully snatched it away: *whack!* "Man, much as that hurt, I popped right up, 'cause I wanted to kill ya, but, soon as I turned to look, you were already halfway up the stairs. I yelled bloody blue murder at you, but when I was done, I thought, little shit is fast, though!" Thereafter, whether calling me home for dinner from the lot in Broad Channel or toasting me at my wedding, my father never referred to me as "Tara" again. "Yup, Scooter, that's how you got your nickname."

And my pièce de résistance, the third installment in this trilogy of two-year-old terror: the infamous shower debacle of 1982. Whenever my mother needed a shower but was taking care of me on her own, her routine was to plunk me into a playpen she wedged in the doorway of our bathroom. Then she'd hop into the tub and spend a minute trying to find that perfect point where the curtain was closed enough to keep the water from getting out but open enough that she could still see me. One particular day it looked something like this: she gave herself a quick rinse, then checked that I was there. She put shampoo in her hair, then checked that I was there. She rinsed out the shampoo, baby's still there. She put conditioner in her hair, baby's there. She rinsed it out, no baby. She ripped open the curtain. No baby! She leaped out of the shower. NO BABY!

In a panic, she snatched a towel from the rack and ran into the living room, where she still didn't see me, but instead saw that way down at the other end of our house a small stool had been pulled up near the back door, which was swinging open in the breeze. With the shower still running and her soaking wet, wearing nothing but a towel, she darted out that door and into our backyard, only to find that the fence gate was also wide open. Now frenzied, Mom ran out into the street, where finally she spotted me, halfway down the block, running full steam toward the intersection.

Living up to my nickname, I was pretty fast even at two, and, given my good head start, my mother struggled to catch up, especially since she couldn't get to full speed while still using one hand to hold up her towel. So, in what may be the world's only example of maternal-instinct-driven streaking, she dropped the towel and sprinted, buck naked, in full view of our Queens street.

Mom caught me just before I stepped off the curb. Not that there was any real danger anymore—by then the street was a parking lot of stopped cars, guys honking, whistling, and cheering like Christmas had come early. She did the only thing she could think of at the time, which was to use my body to hide hers, like a toddler turned fig leaf. And then she walked backward, carrying me in her arms, until we made it to the discarded towel.

My parents' nine-year marriage would convert, in "Catholic years," to all of about three minutes. Plus, my father being one of seven children, and my mother being one of six, the fact that I am an only child is nearly statistically impossible for Catholics. I cannot exist. I do, of course, but I am the first and only only child in the history of both sides of my family.

Because I was just two years old when my parents split, I've never known them together. The consolation for that is, *I've never known them together.* Those old, dark days of two rough jobs, too little money, too much drink, and too little in common were only ever spoken about reluctantly, in dribs and drabs, after a lot of prodding, when I was well into adulthood. And the few photos that exist of my parents during their marriage capture only their rosiest moments.

Those pictures weren't dug up from the bottom of long-buried shoeboxes until I was a teenager. Seeing them for the first time gave me a smile, quickly cut short by a queasy "oh, shit" feeling I can only liken to seeing photos of happy people waving to the crowd as they pull away from port onboard a great ship you then realize is the *Titanic*.

Eventually I was charmed by the photos, finding, however ironically, that seeing my parents in the early days of their marriage was a pretty satisfying source of closure—the official portrait of my dad, baby-faced with a side part, in his police blues; the three-part series of my mom in a tight pair of bellbottoms kneeling in a field plucking daisies; the shot of them holding hands and flashing smiles as they led the recessional out of St. Francis Xavier; him mid-dive in a pair of belted short-short swim trunks; all ninety pounds of her climbing a pool ladder; and the two of them together on a balcony overlooking the beach, him bare-chested beneath a fully unbuttoned short-sleeve guayabera shirt, her in a halter-top bikini, his right arm disappearing behind her back, a half-smoked cigarette and a half-full glass in his left hand raised in a toast to the camera.

6

My mother met Mark for the very first time in a conference room at a Detroit hotel. She was a ball of nerves in a red skirt suit, arranging tent cards and glasses of water on the table for the clients and wondering when he would arrive.

Having cleaned his apartment for over a year, she knew he was a tall man from the size of the suits in his closet, but still, she was in shock when he walked in—he had steel-blue eyes, reeked of intelligence, and stood six feet, ten inches tall.

She had just taken the job as his administrative assistant. The position was very part-time—two or three days a month—and required traveling to big cities around the country. Mark was a business consultant with a growing clientele, and he needed some on-the-road assistance, particularly to set up his conference rooms and film his presentations. Mom had done very little traveling in her life and was thrilled at the chance to see new places.

They had dinner together that first night, and, as my mom describes it, all "the bells and whistles went off" for her. By the second night of the trip it was clear that there was a mutual attraction.

They dated very casually at first, but Mom still felt she shouldn't be in his employ anymore. She took a waitressing job and saw Mark every other weekend, when I was with my father. But by the time I was four, some three years after her first day as his cleaning lady, there was no denying that they were in love.

When my mom decided to quit working for Mark after they started dating, it was for two clear reasons. Reason one was my grandfather's legendary mantra, which she first heard at sixteen. It was her inaugural day working with him at the Yankee Stadium concession stand, and he had been showing her the ropes for so long, he was down to strings—this ursine man in an apron, trying his best to be dead serious yet unable to shake his trademark ear-to-ear grin and sweet, singsong delivery:

"Oh! And angle the cup when you pour the beer so

you don't get too much foam—people want their money's worth!

"And don't put too many peanuts in the bag that you can't twist the top closed—they'll lose half of 'em before they get back to their seats!

"And for CRYIN' OUT LOUD, remember, management counts the cups!! No freebies!" It was the fourth time he had brought up "the cups," and for a second she lost focus, so he started chomping his pair of tongs open and closed in the air to get her attention. When she turned to face him, in a single, superfast swoop he plucked two hot dogs off the row of rolling rods with his right hand, landed them smack in the middle of their respective buns in his left, winked, and said, "All work is honorable, Carmella."

Reason two was that, while the clanging of the tongs still rang true in her ears, on top of that—for her—working was more than an honor; it was a hard-won dream. She was the first woman in the history of her family to want a career, the second to finish high school, and the sole person—male or female—to earn a college degree. Waiting tables until the want ads proffered a better use of that degree was fine by her, especially since she had fought so hard to avoid the alternative—i.e., *not* working. Her mother didn't understand why she wanted to go to college in the first place, then strongly encouraged her to drop out when she and my father got engaged in her junior year. After I was born, despite the fact that my parents were barely scraping by on my father's salary alone, my dad didn't want her to go back to work either. So, in the end, that Mark was in a position to pay her way was not nearly as impressive to my mom as the fact that he knew her well enough never to offer.

Like my mother, Mark was divorced, and their decision not to marry or live together full-time was born of two consequent, shared philosophies: "been there/done that/didn't work" and "see each other on the weekends, read books in between."

More than anything else, though, when it came to raising me, my mom felt that in order to fully do it her way, it had to be fully on her dime. So, that's why she went on to live a dual life: weekdays in Queens, weekends at Mark's duplex on Roosevelt Island or his home in the Hamptons, back and forth week after week, month after month. And every other weekend I was right there with her—the two of us like superwomen, able to jump social strata in a single bound!

Like all Hamptons-goers, the very first thing I did when I got to Mark's country estate was peruse the grounds. Unlike any other Hamptons-goer in the history of Hamptons-going, I did not do so by strolling about draped in white linen and dangling a goblet of Chablis, but by way of a blue plastic Power Wheels 4x4 pickup with a windshield decal that read HIGH RIDER.

As a young tomboy with a mussed pageboy haircut, legs covered in black-and-blues, and a perpetual Dalí dirt mustache, that "truck" was to me what the antique porcelain vase was to my mother. Mark had bought it for me at the Bridgehampton Caldor (think Target of the 1980s) after I hopped over the door of the display model straight into the driver's seat, one-handed the steering wheel, and stuck my bent elbow out the window like a kindergarten cowboy. He and my mother laughed all the way to the cash register. Then they let me drive out of the store. Even with the pedal to the metal I trailed several feet behind as they *walked* through the parking lot, but I was in heaven anyway, inching past rows of vintage convertible Benzes and brand new Saab 900s with my head held high, maxing it out at 3 mph.

Since I had first received my Power Wheels pickup, Mark always had it charged up and ready for me to ride whenever I arrived. He parked it right next to the front door of the Main House—forty bucks' worth of glittery, '80s blue plastic with flame decals, faux monster-truck tires, a "chrome" front, and a row of *frog* lights lining the roll bar (it would be ten years before I learned they were called *fog* lights—they looked like frogs' eyes!), standing sentinel over a million-dollar, five-bedroom, immaculately restored early 1900s farmhouse that was once on the cover of *House Beautiful* magazine.

I was seven the day I ran out of the limo into my mother's outstretched arms as she screamed "Chickenellahh!!" The second I saw my truck, I wriggled out of my mom's bear hug and took off running. It could take me upward of two hours to do my standard full sweep of the property, both because I made countless stops, and because HIGH RIDER and I moved at a slower pace than most people walked. So for the trek Mom always packed me a picnic lunch: a red-checkered blanket, a thermos of orange juice, and a sandwich wrapped in a paisley cloth napkin (at his country home, Mark used only this type of napkin, otherwise known to me as a bandana, and for years I would crack myself up thinking that my little turkey and cheese belonged on Axl Rose's head). I checked the "trunk" to be sure my lunch was there, and right before

I hit the gas, I put on my full-face, adult-size motorcycle helmet.

On another trip to Caldor I had snatched said helmet off a shelf and gone running toward a mirror to see myself with it on. It was so big and heavy that as soon as I pulled it over my tiny head, I went face-first into the glass. After that initial hit, I bounced backward, and within seconds my scrawny body was trailing my gigantic helmeted noggin, like some possessed real-life marionette, careening headlong into racks of cheap ladies' blouses and chintzy sweaters. Once again, Mark laughed his way to the cash register and bought it for me.

By now, I knew better how to handle my gear. I palmed both sides of the helmet as I ever so slowly lowered it over my head, keeping a tight grip to steady my swaying neck until I found that sweet equilibrium, and then off I went—a little girl exploring a Bridgehampton estate in a muscle-tee on a Fisher-Price variety of a "good ol' boy" pickup truck, sporting a cocksure smile under a helmet so enormous it engulfed both my head and neck and came to rest on my shoulders, making me look like a bobblehead doll the second I moved an inch.

The whole of Mark's property was one acre (a football field, including end zones), but it might as well have been the Sahara to me. At no more than twenty feet away from the front door, I already felt worlds away from everything and everyone I knew, as if I were truly on an epic solo adventure. I headed straight for the farthest edge of the grounds, where an old split-rail wood fence separated Mark's property from a potato field that stretched beyond the horizon. Once there, I ditched the helmet and truck, stepped up onto the first rung of the fence, and pushed down on the top rail with my arms to bring myself onto my tiptoes, stretching as high as I could and tilting my head all the way back so the maximum amount of breeze would blow through my hair. If I spotted a potato or two that had eluded the harvesting machine, I ducked under the fence, scurried over and back with lightning speed, and hid them in my "glove box" along with the rest of my secret stashes from earlier trips. I prized the spuds that much more for being weeks old and covered in gnarly sprouts (with regard to my seven-year-old fascination level, gnarly potato sprouts were second only to the Overhead Control Panel).

The field was owned by Mrs. Grace Talmadge, a Bridgehampton native whose family had farmed the land for generations and who had once owned Mark's property as well her own smaller plot right next door. She was a widow in her eighties and the quintessential crotchety, nosy neighbor, forever peering over the hedges in an oversize sun hat, but she didn't at all mind my taking the leftover potatoes—the Artful Dodger act was just my idea of fun.

After the grand potato heist, I got back into the truck and headed along the western edge of the property to pass the fifty-foot row of giant honeysuckle and wisteria bushes. They were skyscraper height in ratio to me in my truck, and I liked to ride as close to them as possible, reaching out a hand to touch their lavender and white blooms as I rolled by, lifting the visor on my helmet to take exaggerated whiffs of the air the way my mom would do, on foot, sans motorcycle helmet.

My mother was long obsessed with flowers and gardening, but she'd never had a garden to garden until she met Mark. On her very first trip to his Bridgehampton place, as he cooked dinner, she headed out to cut some blooms from those very bushes. At the time they were the only flowering plants on the grounds, but over the coming days, as he saw the vases in his house fill up with her arrangements and she told him about all the time she spent as a kid at the Brooklyn Botanic Garden, he took her to a local nursery and gave her carte blanche to plant whatever, wherever she wanted. And in the three years since—with the help of a ropy-armed, tan, leather-skinned landscaper named John Bell, who would soon become a good friend—she rained down flowers on that place in a joy-driven frenzy, putting in boatloads of potted plants, a couple of vine-covered trellises, a school-bus-size patch of hydrangeas smack in the middle of the rear lawn, and rings of flowers around anything that didn't move. On her more manic planting days, it felt as if, if you kept still for too long, you might look down to find yourself standing inside a circle of tulips.

My favorite of all the flower beds was her wildest creation, a Technicolor jumble of towering hollyhocks, hibiscus, allium, and gladiolas, brimming with bees and butterflies, which happened to frame the front entrance of the next stop on my tour, the Barn. Though it had once been a fully functional, classic, big red wooden barn, Mark had since turned it into one huge sitting room. He put in a proper wooden floor, added paned windows and double glass doors on the westernmost side, and faced all the chairs and sofas in that direction for watching the sunset. At sundown, it was truly the most wonderful place to be, but being alone in there at midday, when the sun sat in the east and it was dim inside, was a whole other story.

While the Barn's primary purpose was for sitting and watching sunsets, it doubled as Mark's very own funhouse. In there he kept his most bizarre furnishings and objets d'art, from the fun and quirky—a hand-carved bald eagle about my height; a gigantic wicker chair, with a seven-foot-high wingback that curled at the top like a question mark and that had circular glass portholes along it (the purpose of this chair eluded even Mark); and a twelve-foot replica of a schoolchild's yellow wooden ruler—to the downright ominous: a pair of five-foot-tall matching brass urns; several horror-movie-quality rocking chairs covered in cobwebs; a couple of cattle yokes hanging on a wall; a twelve-branch candelabra with decades' worth of wax dripping down like a waterfall stopped in time, adhering it permanently to the wormwood table on which it sat; and an actual church confessional—a ten-foot-tall wooden box with a little door and creepy, rattan-covered windows to obscure the face of the person confessing sins.

As always, I did a stroll of the perimeter, dragging a dusty finger along the tables and chairs as I moved in super slow-mo to avoid making the floor creak and averting my eyes from the scary stuff for as long as I could. Finally I would give in, stopping and letting my gaze dart around the room: *rocking chair, cattle yoke, urns*—spin around on my heels with a, "Hello? Anybody there?"—*candelabra, cobwebs, confessional.* Once I'd made it that far, I upped the ante and challenged myself to see how long I could sit inside the confessional, and after ten seconds I upped the ante even further by deciding to actually confess, "For-give me, Father—*deep breath*—for I have sinned—*you're okay*—I have taken more potatoes.... AHHHHHH!" I ran straight out of there, then right out the back door of the Barn, collapsing onto the grass outside in a heap, arms crossed, rubbing away my goose bumps in a patch of sun at the foot of the Cottage.

The three structures on Mark's property were arranged in a triangle. The Main House was on the northeastern side, the Barn was on the southwestern side, and tucked at the northwestern corner was the Cottage. The smallest of the three, the Cottage was still twice the size of my Broad Channel boat shed, with a separate bedroom, a combo living/dining room, and a small galley kitchen. There couldn't have been a more charming guesthouse, but I had little reason to spend much time inside it, with two excep-tions: the first was when it rained. Because the Cottage had a thin roof and exposed-wood walls, you could hear the distinct *ping* or *plop* of every raindrop, and as soon as those first drops fell, Mark would have us stop whatever we were doing and rush over there, the three of us sitting in total silence, eyes closed, ears perked, listening to the rain as if it were Schubert's *Impromptus.*

The second reason was for my personal Wild West reenactments.

When I finally shook off the willies and got onto my feet, I headed straight into the Cottage for some much-needed, confidence-boosting, cowboy role-play. Nothing in the decor would have suggested that this was the place to do that, save one very important element (the magnificence of which was often lost on the adults who spent any time in there), and that was the pair of swinging saloon doors that separated the kitchen from the living room.

I started with the slow John Wayne slide through: "Well, howdy, partner." Then on to the preeminent grab-and-pull, followed by double quick draw: "Stick 'em up!" And finally an anachronistic kung-fu-movie-style ninja pounce, followed by three minutes of Bruce Lee meets grand mal seizure karate chops and rapid-fire roundhouse kicks. All in all, I probably busted through those doors a dozen more times that day, changing up the style with each go before the road called, and with a tip of the imaginary hat, I was on my way.

For the first year I visited Mark's country place, from ages four to five, the grassy, low-grade hill that was the communal yard among the three houses held nothing but the twenty-buck vinyl kiddie pool I begged him for—it was the type you filled with a garden hose, about the size of your average round kitchen table, with little cartoon animals printed along the outside, and it was so out of place and scale on this picturesque, roving lawn, seeing it was like stumbling upon a plastic-frosted toy donut on a moor in *Wuthering Heights*. And while Mark found the image of my Power Wheels truck next to his historic farmhouse comical in its absurdity, the baby pool just pissed him off. So one day he decided to put in a real pool.

Two years and God only knows how many tens of thousands of dollars later, where once there was a little ring of plastic holding a bathtub's worth of cold water in the middle of a giant field of grass, there was now an entire stonework, lagoon-inspired pool that, as Mark had hoped, most people refused to believe wasn't a nature-made pond. He didn't want to level the land, so one side was ten feet high, made of many hundreds of pieces of hand-laid slate, a sort of castle wall built into the earth. In lieu of a standard metal ladder with railings was an intentionally askew pile of descending giant gray stones at one end by which you could get in or out of the water. And he asked my mother to plant all sorts of dangly, weeping flowers around the perimeter, their leaves and blooms grazing the water's edge as if they had been there for a hundred years. Naturally, pool toys were strictly forbidden. (I complained about this for years, entirely unable to comprehend that not having a neon-orange foam noodle was a small price to pay for having my own fucking lagoon. In fact, I hadn't even realized until writing this that, in essence, he built the thing for me.)

However incredible the pool was, because I saw it every other weekend in the summer, and because it was now lunchtime, not pool time, after my gunslinger/Jackie Chan escapade in the Cottage, I merrily cruised by it in my truck without as much as a passing glance, on my way to have my turkey and cheese sandwich by the croquet court.

Mark was a self-made guy who, as might already be somewhat obvious, had decided to skip the whole nouveau riche thing and go full steam ahead to "old money." And so, where someone else of his means might have put in a tennis court, he opted for a regulation, English-style croquet court—for the internationally competitive game that is played on the putting-green-short grass of a lawn about half the size of a soccer field, studded with rectangular wickets only a hairsbreadth wider than the balls you knock through them using a three-foot-tall wooden mallet. That's all to say, it was a shit-ton different from the boxed-up backyard version anyone I've ever met might be familiar with.

I set up camp just outside the perimeter of the court at the far end, one-handing my sandwich as I leaned forward to focus in on Mark, who was lining up to take a shot from the opposite corner. He looked like a grandfather clock at this distance—20 percent clock face (his head and torso) and 80 percent pendulum (the mallet swinging past the stilts that were his legs). The ball came flying in my direction, and Mark followed it, covering thirty yards of ground in four strides. He was still a good car's length away from me on my picnic blanket, but his shadow cast a Mack truck's worth of shade, and in it we could see each other clearly. I gave him a wave, and he gave me a nod, and then he went right back to croquet practice—this wasn't the time to talk, but there would be plenty of that later on.

There was a rhythm to life here, an unspoken, unofficial schedule that took us through each hour of each weekend in nearly the same way from one summer to the next to the next. I would pack up my picnic supplies and drive my truck back to the front of the Main House. Mark would finish croquet practice, Mom would wrap up her gardening, and, depending on the weather, we would go for a swim or head into town to go antiquing. We might hit the outdoor show at the Bridgehampton Elks Club or

Mom and Mark's favorite shop in Sag Harbor or Camps', which I think was the name of the couple who owned it, and I would play with their shaggy white sheepdog while Mom and Mark bought more wormwood tables or porcelain pitchers or cattle yokes.

When we got back, we'd start preparing dinner, me on a stool in between Mom and Mark at the kitchen counter, the three of us shucking corn and clams assembly-line style. But no matter how far along we got, we would stop at five o'clock on the nose to have cocktails in the Barn. We chatted away until the lavender hour, at which point we would fall into a trance, robotically raising and lowering our respective gin and tonics and chocolate milks to our mouths without even looking down at our glasses so as not to miss a second of the sunset.

Dinner was always had in the Main House—on the porch on warm nights, at a small table by the fireplace on cold ones, or in the dining room if we had guests. And after dinner there would always be cognac, pie, and conversation—hours and hours of cosmically impactful conversation.

In the mornings we read newspapers and ate pastries, and then the whole thing started again, until about four o'clock on Sunday. That's when Mark would get into his vintage maroon 1978 Lincoln Continental with white leather interior and vanity plates that read VI X (as in 6'10"), turn on the news or the classical station, and head back to his duplex on Roosevelt Island. And that's when Mom and I would get back into our Cutlass, no vanity plates, blast the Pointer Sisters or Donna Summer, hit the Burger King drive-thru for dinner, and go to our Monday-through-Friday home on 251st Street in Queens.

For the other two weekends a month, I was with my dad—the two of us leaping around a ten-mile radius in south-eastern Queens, from our actual home in Broad Channel to the home of hot roast beef and Skee-Ball in Howard Beach (the Big Bow Wow) to the home of my favorite cousins, TJ and Deanna, and my Pall Mall–smoking, Wrangler-jeans-wearing Uncle Dennis and—finally—to the home-away-from-home of Joey O'Dirt, English Billy, Rodger the Dodger, and my dad: Gregory's Bar and Restaurant.

7

Most regulars at neighborhood bars come by their nicknames through easily distinguishable physical qualities (Curly Pat, Jimmy the Hat, Mumbling Joe, Peg-Leg). If that fails, a nickname can be created on the basis of ethnic origin (English Billy, Irish Mike, and Dutch—just Dutch, because there's never more than one) or a profession (Eddie the Actor; Tugboat, who captained one; and Rodger the Dodger, a defense attorney). But in the entire history of nicknaming, there was only regular called Tara's Father.

Dad started taking me to Gregory's Bar and Restaurant on Metropolitan Avenue in Kew Gardens, Queens, in 1986, when I was six years old. He was single with a kid in tow and looking for love. So, that same year, to really up his odds, he bought himself a white Members Only jacket, a pair of dark-tinted aviator Carrera sunglasses the size of ski goggles, the very latest nylon Nikes with the saw-blade soles, and a brand-new black Chrysler Laser hatchback that talked.

Dad went ahead and splurged on the XE model because it was equipped with: 1) the groundbreaking all-digital dashboard (for me, the biggest thrill of having an odometer that displayed each mile per hour in speed in cutting-edge green boxy font was to scream the fast-rising count aloud every single time Dad took off from a stoplight: "Five, six, seven ... eleven, twelve, thirteen ... twenty-three, twenty-four, twenty five ..." I never once made it higher than thirty before Dad went bananas, screaming, "ENOUGH ALREADY, SCOOTER!!!"); and, 2) the incredible new Electronic Voice Alert System, the height of technology at the time. The owner's manual claimed the car could voice twenty-four different warning messages, though I'll be damned if I ever heard more than two. The first seemed to be delivered completely at random. If we'd be cruising down the Belt Parkway on a sunshiney day, singing along to John Mellencamp or Tom Petty, out of nowhere the radio volume would automatically lower—pretty fucking incredible—so the car could provide us with this lifesaving bit of information: "WIPER FLUID LOW!"

The second message I could actually instigate, and, boy, did I.

Probably the first fifty times Dad picked me up from PS 133 in "The Laser" instead of a squad car, I'd pile in a half dozen kids and close the door, only to crack it back open again. "Shh! Listen . . ." I'd say, and after what felt like forever, the car would say, "DOOR AJAR!" and everybody would go batshit. "Whoa!!!!!!!! Make it do it again!!!"

Between the new car and clothes, Dad was really going for broke in the trying-to-get-a-girlfriend department, and I was more than thrilled to be a part of this effort: "Scoot, I tell ya, there ain't nothin' a woman likes more than to see a guy who takes care a' his responsibilities— you're my closer, kiddo! Come to think of it, wouldn't be so bad if you let the pretty ones know that I'm the one who sprays your No More Tangles stuff and combs your hair all nice like I do!"

Tomboy that I was, I ordinarily fought off having my hair brushed as if it was torture. But I knew that my looking good was as important as Dad's looking good when we went to Gregory's, so I always took one for the team. (The rarity of this gesture on my part should be noted. Under no other circumstances—for example, church—did I give a crap about how I looked. To this day, one of my dad's favorite stories is the time that he told me I could go outside in my Easter Sunday dress to wait in front of the house while he got ready. Before I stepped out the door, he wagged a finger in my face for a good ten seconds and told me, over and over again, that I was absolutely NOT to play in the dirt or grass. He came out five minutes later and couldn't find me anywhere, until he looked up—I was swinging my legs and bopping my head in bliss, straddling the branch of the tree I had climbed, totally oblivious of the wide stripe of black sap and bark running straight down the front of my white satin dress. Dad was ready to blow a gasket, but right before he did, I cut him off: "You did NOT say anything about the TREE, Dad!" He *but-but-but*ted like a broken-down Broad Channel motorboat for half a minute before finally giving up and storming off. And without another word we walked up Cross Bay to Mass at St. Virgilius; him shaking his head, pissed as all hell at first but getting a tiny bit closer to smiling with each stride; me looking down, feigning regret but holding back a smirk, because I knew by the time we hit the VFW after church, he'd be slapping his leg and laughing like crazy, retelling that story to his buddies: "Little shit had a point—I mean, what the hell's a guy to say? I DIDN'T tell her NOT to go up the goddamn tree!")

In the end, Dad's full-court-press for love paid off—apparently no woman can resist a well-groomed, pint-size wing-girl coupled with a grown man doing a David Hasselhoff as Michael Knight impression—and by the end of 1986 he was seriously dating one of the Gregory's waitresses, a recent Irish transplant named Jackie. From then on out, he was at the bar every weekend. And on the weekends when I wasn't driving High Rider around Mark's Bridgehampton estate, I was right there with him.

After a couple of years of such weekends, getting ready to go to Gregory's on a Saturday night had become a ritual:

Right around three o'clock the screen door of our Broad Channel house thwacks open a split second before the unmistakable two-note blast of Dad's double-pinky "C'mere!" whistle rings out across the land (my guess would be that it could be heard all the way from the Call-A-Head Porta Potties to about fifty feet offshore on Jamaica Bay). I stop dead in my tracks and hop over a fence or scurry down a tree or drop the ball mid-game or turn whatever little rickety skiff Tommy O'Reilly and I have stolen that day right around and start rowing back to shore with him pissing and moaning the whole way, or some combination of all four, and get my ass home.

"Okay, Scooter, time for the three S's!" Dad says when I come in, which I know means, "Shit, Shower, Shave," so I giggle, and he lifts one eyebrow and teases, "What?!" and I giggle some more, and he winks and whispers "Don't you say it now!" and I don't, but hearing my dad curse in conversation with me, even in acronym, makes me feel like the most badass seven-year-old on God's green Earth.

Standing shirtless in a tight pair of Levi's with a cigarette in his teeth, Dad lays out my clothes on our pilly brown pullout couch, stares at them a second, crinkles his nose, squeezes his Salem into a groove in the ashtray so he can use both hands to "press" my shirt and pants with his palm-irons, then heads for the bathroom, where, forgetting about the still-lit original cigarette, he lights another, which I take as my cue to sneak a puff off the first.

I step out of my old clothes and throw on my new ones in no time, then plop down on the couch waiting for Dad to finish up with the S's. In two seconds I'm bored, so I call to him in the shower:

"Eh, Da!!"

"What?"

"Is *asshole* a curse?"

"TA-RA!"

"Sorry!"

Pause.

"Um, Da?"

"Yes?"

"What about *bastard*?"

"Tara Elizabeth! When I get out of here . . ."

"Okay, okay, I got it!"

"You'd better have 'got it'! Now bring me my Norelco, will ya?!"

I roll my eyes and let my body slip lifelessly off the couch all the way to the floor. Once there, I do a good bit of melodramatic writhing around on the carpet before finally lumbering up onto my feet and huffing and puffing over to his dresser. And then I stop. And stare. Like it's the very first time I'm seeing them, like I can even remember a time they weren't there . . .

For the extent of my life thus far and stretching ahead for at least the next twenty-odd years, no matter where my dad roams, the top of his dresser always holds the same series of items: one Norelco brand electric shaver standing upright in its charger, one gold chain necklace with three charms—a crucifix, one that reads #1 DAD, and a round gold medallion with a miniature silver replica of his police badge in the middle—one black leather flip case with his actual police badge inside; one bottle of Paco Rabanne cologne; one men's Speed Stick musk deodorant; his money clip; one classic black acrylic comb; a little pile of loose change; and two .38 Smith & Wesson military- and police-issue revolvers.

Those guns live on top of my dad's dresser the way the Cocoa Puffs live on top of the fridge, the way my little lineup of Hot Wheels lives on the window ledge, the way I live here and in my grandparents' basement and in a Bridgehampton mansion all at the same time, and this is just how things are and how things always have been, and I don't think much about any of it, until I do, and I guess that all started with the guns.

"Scooter?!" Dad yells from right behind me, and by the look on his face when I finally turn away from the dresser to face him, it seems he's been calling me for a while.

"Scooter?!!"

"Oh, hey, Da."

"You okay?"

"Yeah."

"I been waitin' on that shaver!"

"Right, sorry."

Dad gives me a puzzled once-over, then shrugs it off,

takes the Norelco, heads back to the bathroom, shaves, comes out, pulls an undershirt on over his head, tucks it in, ties his shoes, straps on his brown leather ankle holster, then his hip holster, opens the top dresser drawer and takes out his bullets, sees me still standing in the same spot, and stops. "You know what? How 'bout you pop a squat, kiddo?"

I take a seat at our kitchen table, and Dad lays his .38s down in front of me. He nods and pats the front pocket of his jeans to make the bullets in them jingle and let me know that the guns are unloaded and it's all right, but I'm not convinced. So he gives the approval: "It's all right." Which doesn't work.

He tries again, "Go ahead, Scooter, pick 'em up."

There is no locked-bottom-drawer-of-the-mahogany-desk-in-the-study in our house. There is no study. There is no desk. In a three-hundred-square-foot, room-divider-less, closet-less former boat shed, problems can't hide; they are right out there with your deodorant and your Paco Rabanne and your kid, day and night. And at some point, there is no way around them but to pick 'em up.

I'm so short that as I slide the guns toward me on the tabletop, they are almost parallel with my eyes. Just before they reach the table's edge, I take a breath, tighten up my grip, and give one last tug. The weight of the guns surprises the shit out of me, and I let out a *whoa!* as they start to dip down, despite my intention of lifting them up. I finally steady my hands and get them going in the right direction. And I don't stop until I'm in full-on touchdown pose.

Dad now gives slow, careful instructions:

"Point them down." I do.

"Get your fingers away from the trigger." I do.

"Now put 'em back on the table." I do.

"And don't ever touch 'em again." I don't. Ever.

8

Even on days when I don't wave two guns over my head like Billy the Kid, Dad and I always play Gene Pitney's cowboy classic, "The Man Who Shot Liberty Valance," on the ride to Gregory's, and today is no different.

We're not even halfway through Howard Beach on Cross Bay when I start begging Dad to cue up the tape. He gives in by the next stoplight, and we take our positions—I sit shotgun with both hands on the imaginary pistols in my imaginary hip holsters. He drives, with one hand on the wheel and the other on the actual gun in his actual hip holster. Then we sing. We know the whole song from the beginning, but it's the chorus we're waiting for, because that's when we do our quick-draw:

The man who shot Liberty Valance, BANG!

He shot Liberty Valance, BANG!

He was the bravest of them all!

Then we play it again, and again, and maybe one more time before Dad flips the tape to play "Town Without Pity." Part of our game here is that I feign hating this song, so he sings it loudly at me and laughs, and I open up my window all the way and try to stick my head out, which just makes him sing louder, and then I can't help myself, and I laugh and join in for the finale, *What a town without pity caaaaaaan do!* "All right, Scoot," Dad finally says, "Howsabout a li'l Creedence now?!"

"Yeah!" After I hand him the tape, I try to kick my heels up onto the dash, but they keep falling short, and though Dad would have been mad had I made it, my failed attempt at coolness cracks him up.

After all that it takes roughly three Punch Buggy punches ("Punch Buggy yellow! *I got you first!* No, I got you first!"), a dozen License Plate Game spottings ("New Jersey! *Easy.* Arkansas!! *Whoa, good one!*"), and one round of Name the State Capitals to get to Gregory's. In other words, twenty minutes.

Since Dad started dating Jackie, two years ago now, we no longer have to hunt for a metered spot on Metropolitan. We pull right into the super-secret employee lot around back, which is neither super nor secret, and, since we park there and so do a few other regulars, it's not even employees only. Still, in my mind it is always the "super-secret employee lot," and getting to park in there is mind-blowingly exciting, both because Dad always makes a big deal out of it—"How'd ya like that, Scoot? Door-to-door service for us!"—and because, unlike your typical suburban parking lot, this one is a Queens special. That is, it is not a flat cement square or rectangle with lines delineating spaces, but a post-earthquake-quality cracked basin of asphalt at the bottom of a driveway with such a steep drop that halfway down you feel as if you're riding on the back of Greg Louganis, mid—nose dive.

There's room for about a half dozen cars in the lot, but there are never fewer than ten in there, squeezed in at impossible angles, back to front and front to back, all of them partially blocking the others and making it inevitable that every hour someone will walk through the bar screaming out a laundry list of cars that need to be moved: "Whoever's got the red Pontiac, the blue Chevy, the black Buick, the green Olds, the tan Nissan, the gray Honda, and the white Toyota needs to move 'em, pronto!" At which time I would always take off running for the lot, pile up a couple of old produce boxes near the dumpster, and climb on top of them to watch a bunch of half-drunk regulars, big-haired waitresses, and bone-tired kitchen guys in grease-black aprons jockey their cars around and around and around, like a giant-size, real-life game of Tetris, with cursing.

While I may have been the Henry Hill of The Geriatrics of 251st Street in my subverted Copacabana scene, at Gregory's that part belonged entirely to Dad.

We hop out of the Laser and slam our doors, a bit too hard and in tandem for effect, and just before we head in, Dad crouches down, pulls his comb from his back pocket, and fixes his part and mustache in the side-view mirror. When he pops back up, he flips the keys over the hood without as much as a sidelong look in my direction and gives me the *nice one* nod when I catch them. I twirl the key ring around my finger as we walk toward the door, feeling even cooler now than I did when he cursed (in acronym) in front of me earlier.

Gregory's back door opens to a long, low-ceilinged, wood-paneled hallway. To your immediate right is the first of two kitchen entryways, and if you cut left, there's a row of pay phones and the johns. Dad smacks the shoulder of some guy on the phone, slaps the back of another one coming out of the bathroom, then pokes his head through the swinging doors of the first kitchen entrance to say hi to the cooks, "Emerico! How goes it pal?!" Then we walk five paces, and Dad sticks his head through the second kitchen entrance to do the same with the dishwashers and busboys on the other side.

We flatten ourselves against the wall as a couple of waitresses fly by, one-handing their pizza-pie-size brown plastic trays of empties over our heads as Dad gives and gets more hellos. "Sherry, my dear!" *Lookie here, Tara's Father in the house!* "And hello, Miss Katie!" *It's really pumping tonight, honey. Better tell Margie right away if ya wanna sit in the crow's nest—could be a wait!* This news gets Dad an instant elbow to the ribs. "Da, we gotta tell her now!!"

"Cool your jets, Scoot. We'll say our hellos, and then I'll tell her, promise."

The dark, muted hall gives way to a sudden burst of clanking glasses, squawking laughs, wide white flashes of light from the TVs hanging over the bar, and eye-level blips of color from the tabletop Pac-Man machine. For me, those first few steps into Gregory's proper are no less mind-blowing than coming up from the subway tunnel and finding yourself in the middle of Grand Central Terminal ... if the train station were a bar in Queens with twelve-foot-high ceilings and a nautical theme.

If you came into Gregory's through the main entrance, you had to pass under an archway made of two real whalebones, each seven feet tall and touching at the top. After that, the whole space is divided in two by a wall of stacked wooden barrels draped with dusty fishing nets and ropes and dotted with the odd pulley and life preserver.

To one side of the barrel wall is the bar, to the other is the dining room, and smack in the middle is the "crow's nest" table. This is an ordinary round table, but it's surrounded by a shoulder-high fence, perched about five feet in the air on a large "mast," and accessible only by ladder. Naturally, it was my favorite place on Earth.

As always, I track Dad's waist from behind as he weaves through the crowd. Random hands reach down to pinch my cheeks and squeeze my shoulders as I go, and offerings from faceless torsos appear right in front of my eyes, from all angles—a dangling maraschino cherry just fished from somebody's Manhattan, a stack of quarters for Pac-Man, a handful of bar nuts. When we finally make it to the bar, we say hello to our friends stool by stool.

A good chunk of the Gregory's regulars sound like a collection of clichés: English Billy typically came to the bar after a game of tennis, wearing white short-shorts and Tretorns. Joey O'Dirt was Irish American, worked in construction, and drank too much. The hostess chain-smoked Virginia Slims and pumped gin martinis for blood; her name was Marge. The Lemanski brothers were Polish.

Another chunk of regulars escaped stereotypes by a hair. Sal wore painted-on, stonewashed jeans with tucked-in white V-neck T-shirts, and his partner, George, worked for the airlines, but as a baggage handler, not a flight attendant. Likewise, Rob was a crooked-teethed Englishman whose hobby was painting portraits, but his boyfriend, Pete, was a giant Italian American who made his living selling commercial washing machines. And of course there was my dad, a cop with aviator sunglasses and a Tom Selleck mustache but who also had one completely unique accessory: me.

The last bunch defied any and all categorization. Don Jo wore a fedora and linen guayabera shirts, but he was originally from Bombay, not Havana, and he sold high-end lace for a living. Daisy was supertall, practically mute, and had a cartoon-quality handlebar mustache—his real name was never disclosed and his nickname never explained.

But in my mind, no matter how close or far these Gregory's denizens might have come to being archetypes, they were all wholly original, if only because of the unlikely fact that they were all gathered here, forming a kind of family.

Dad sneaks up on Daisy from behind, throwing his left arm around his shoulders and jutting his right in front of his chest, fingers spread, awaiting a handshake. (A move he'll repeat on a good four or five more guys at the bar.) As soon as English Billy sees us coming, he gets up from his stool, then lifts me up to take his place. In no time Kiki, the Swedish bartender, slides over a beer for Dad and an orange and cranberry juice with at least three swizzle sticks for me. Jackie zooms through to give Dad a drive-by kiss before flying back off to check on her tables, while Joey O'Dirt sidles up next to me and puts a couple of quarters on top of my stack, announcing, "I'm gonna kick your ass today, kid!," which gets him a quick flick to the ear from Dad. "Eh!! Watch the language, ya dope!"

Joey and I head over to the tabletop Pac-Man machine while Dad tells Margie to put us down for dinner in the crow's nest. No more than ten minutes later we climb up there to eat. After another ten minutes I have my face pressed between the fence posts with a half-eaten chicken finger clenched in my teeth, pretending I'm a nineteenth-century explorer of the high seas while not so inconspicu-ously looking down people's shirts. Dad is kicking back, popping fries and drinking beer, waving out at the crowd in between sips as though he's the Pope of Gregory's, and the crow's nest table is the popemobile.

Somewhere around 9:00 p.m. we pay our bill, go back out the same way we came in, hop into the Laser, and head home.

This routine happened again and again, every odd Saturday night of my life, for the next five years. And while there was never another night that was kicked off by me waving two guns over my head, there were a couple of more exceptional ones to come. That spring, just before my eighth birthday, Dad threw my First Communion party at Gregory's. And in addition to all the regulars, some combination of my Clancy family was there, too: my Grandma Alice; my uncles Gil, Arthur, Dennis, Thomas, and Michael; my aunts Margaret, Nancy, Linda, Carol, and Kathy; and some number of my twenty-one first cousins, Tricia, Little Gil, Joanie, John, Kathy, Nancy, Little Arthur, Young John, Adam, Colleen, AJ, Audra, Alice, Arlene, Butchie, Deanna, TJ, Little Thomas, Shawn, Danny, and Caitlin. Like a fairy tale, Dad didn't care that I was still wearing my white bride of Jesus dress and new gold crucifix necklace while I played handball with my cousins on the wall next to the deli out front on Metropolitan.

Those young nights weren't all quite so dreamy. More than a few times Dad had too much to drink at Gregory's and would run the red lights on Cross Bay Boulevard on our way home. Just once I said, "Hey, Da, you shouldn't do that." And he shot me a nasty look, to which I said, "I mean, what if the police see us?" He cranked the radio, then screamed a line I'd heard before: "I-AM-THE-POLICE!" I shut my mouth and my eyes, white-knuckling the edges of my seat and taking long, deep, terrified breaths through my nose.

Those white-knuckled nights were somewhat redeemed, however, on Christmas Eve 1989. A few weeks beforehand Dad had sat me down on the couch. "All right, Scooter," he said.

Anxiously I cut him off, in textbook nine-year-old fashion. "Am I in trouble?"

"No, no. It's something good. Do you think I should ask Jackie to marry me?"

I didn't miss a beat. "Yup."

Everything moved pretty fast from there. Dad and I headed over to see Slim—Dad's nickname for his jeweler friend, a thin Armenian with a magnifying loupe hanging permanently below his Adam's apple. With the ring on order, he conferred with the Gregory's crew: Marge, Daisy, Don Jo, English Billy, Joey O'Dirt, the Lemanski brothers, Kiki, the waitresses Katie and Sherry, Pete and Rob, and George and Sal, who were organizing the Christmas Eve party.

The night of the party, English Billy picked me up early, giving my dad some time alone with Jackie to pop the question. When the two of them came through the door, hand in hand, Gregory's erupted in cheers.

A few months later Gregory's Bar and Restaurant took over the entire coach section of a Dublin-bound Aer Lingus 747, en route to the wedding in Ireland. This was back when you could smoke on planes, and, more important, it was back when they gave out unlimited free booze. Everyone was standing up in the aisles, telling jokes and clinking glasses. A little nautical decoration and they might never have left that plane.

The bridal party was an even split of staff and regulars. As the flower girl, I led the lot of them into the church. Jackie, her dress adorned with top-quality lace (a wedding gift from Don Jo), walked slowly down the aisle, past pews full of the entire hungover, ragtag Queens crew, and met Dad at the altar.

After the wedding, Dad and I moved out of our little Broad Channel house and into a two-bedroom railroad apartment in nearby Richmond Hill, Queens, with Jackie, marking a minuscule gain in actual square footage but an exponential one with regard to rooms with doors that closed.

Later that year, 1990, Dad officially retired from the NYPD. He was only forty years old, but he had already put in twenty-two years on the job and was entitled to a full retirement pension, not that he intended on kicking up his heels. He had started going to college at night, six years earlier, after a major off-duty scare:

As an unmarried man with no other children, he had only one true Achilles' heel—me. And once, we ran into someone he had put away. Having served his sentence, the guy was out doing what we were doing at the time, shopping for clothes, a seemingly innocuous thing to do. But when my father saw the man's face across the suit racks, he instantly pulled one of his guns from its holster. Then, without a word, he took my wrist and shoved me behind a nearby cash register. The two men locked eyes, and the guy nodded. "Hi, Clancy." Hiding the gun in his hand behind a row of suits, my dad said hello back.

"It's gotta be fifteen years. You just out?" my father said.

"Yeah, 'fraid so."

"You were only supposed to do seven to nine. Must not have been such a good boy in there, huh?"

"Nope. But I'm back with my wife now. She had two more kids while I was in!"

"Immaculate Conceptions, huh?"

They laughed.

The guy didn't seem an immediate threat. But when they parted ways, as the ex-con kept thumbing through the rack, my dad slowly walked off, leaving the clothes behind and grabbing me just before we reached the door.

A week later Dad started taking accounting classes at Queens College.

Six years after that he traded his life as a warrant-squad cop for a desk job at H&R Block—pretty damn likely making him the only person in the world whose career path reads: aspiring priest, bounty hunter, accountant.

And yet, of all the varying titles he held, Dad always made it clear to me, if only in his pick-up-the-guns/ three *S*'s/red light–running/mustache and aviator glasses– wearing way, that there was one title that forever trumped all the others: Tara's Father.

9

In 1990, right after my dad married Jackie and moved out of our Broad Channel house, my hard-ass grandmother somehow wound up moving in with her Wall Street daughter and son-in-law and their three kids in the most elite of New York City suburbs, while Mom and I stayed in Queens, in a new house, two blocks away, on 253rd Street. (Grandpa refused to stop working at MetLife in Brooklyn, so Mom bought a bunk bed for my room, and from Monday to Friday I took the top and he took the bottom.) I wasn't there when my grandmother said good-bye to the other Geriatrics of 251st Street, but I'd bet good money that it went something like this:

"My youngest, Lucille, fancy she is now! Connecticut, she wants to live?! What do I know from Connecticut?!

But she needs me, for the kids! I'm gonna let a stranger, some *sfacimm* 'nanny' or what they call it, watch my grand-kids?! My blood! I'd rather be dead! So that's it, *fahn-gool!* . . . good-bye." Then I imagine a rope ladder dropping down from a hovering helicopter, the blasting propeller winds matting down Tina's and Anna's Aqua-Netted helmets of hair, and Grandma hooking an elbow around the lowest rung, lifting into the sky in her threadbare, floral-print, pale orange housedress and dangling terry-cloth slippers, flying up over the clotheslines of eastern Queens, and fi-nally being deposited onto my Aunt Lucille's manicured front lawn in Westport, Connecticut, right in between the gobsmacked landscaper holding on to his leaf blower for dear life and the petrified neighbor with a popped-collar polo and pearls who had just come over to deliver a batch of welcome-to-the-neighborhood scones.

To say that the simultaneous loss of my hero grandmother, Tommy O'Reilly, and the rest of my Broad Channel pals, along with the two homes I had grown up in, would make me come untethered would imply that I had ever been tethered in the first place. By then, age ten, I was already a tried-and-true child chameleon, a real-life little Zelig who knew how to go from being barfly at a Queens local hangout to a summertime Bridgehamptonite to an honorary septuagenarian at the drop of a dime. Despite all that (or maybe because of it), there was one role I didn't always like to play: kid. More specifically, rule-abiding kid.

According to my parents, from kindergarten right on up, they never went more than a month without getting a call from my school's principal. I would leave class "to go to the bathroom" and not come back for an hour—I'd hit the office to shoot the breeze with the school secretary, then move on to the school nurse, and then the security guard. If they were new, I'd pull my trademark, "So, you got any kids?" And if I knew them already, I'd ask how little Kevin was doing these days or what they thought about them Mets, as if I were Dad making the rounds at Gregory's. (It typically took a few minutes before whomever I was talking to copped on that I was not supposed to be there chitchatting and would shoo me back off to class—not that I went.)

I had a particular infatuation with the "secret" fourth floor of PS 133, and I'd sneak up there, climb under the yellow caution tape, and have a nice long snoop around (it was quarantined due to asbestos contamination for my entire six years of elementary school). After that tour I'd pop my head into the gym, and if the coast was clear, I'd slip past the door and start running loops around the perimeter as fast as I could to practice for my recess races against the boys, or I'd take the California Raisins figurines our gym teacher, Ms. Lobasco, would give us as rewards for doing the President's Challenge Fitness Test's recommended number of sit-ups for our age and gender, line them up at half-court, and then bowl them over with a basketball (imaginary giant snowball), screaming, "AVALANCHE!!" And whether I was caught and taken back to class by the hand, or on the rare occasion when I went of my own volition, I was placed in a special desk right next to the teacher's so that he or she could keep me from telling jokes to my neighbor, or yank me back down to my seat when I stood up on my chair and did the hula to get a rise out of my classmates.

It's impossible to say whether my refusal to sit still or listen to the rules was more the product of nature or nurture, but I would guess that at least some part of it stemmed from the fact that I spent so much of my time outside of school adapting to multiple, very different adult worlds. Once I was in school, I must have decided that everyone could just adapt to me. Which is likely why, for nearly the whole first half of elementary school, I didn't have many close friends. It would go something like this: *"Hey, Tara, want to help us build a house with the blocks?"* "Nah. You wanna cut class, sneak onto the cordoned-off fourth floor, and breathe in a little asbestos?! No? Well, to hell with ya."

But then, along came Esther . . .

Despite her having a name that suggests she was an eighty-five-year-old Jewish grandmother, Esther Hilsenrad and I first met as fellow third-graders. We sat at least three rows away from each other—or however many bodies it took to get alphabetically from Clancy to Hilsenrad in a packed Queens public-school classroom—but for at least the first half of the school year, I'm sure she wished we were even farther apart.

Esther and I were not just of a different species; we were of a different genus. I was Catholic. She was Jewish. I was the shortest kid in the class. She was the tallest. I didn't shut up. She barely said a word. I kept dog-eared notebooks full of chicken-scratch handwriting and had a permanent seat in the principal's office. She had pristine notebooks and was petrified of getting into trouble. I had the confidence-bordering-on-arrogance typical of only children, while she had the frenetic look in her eye typical of anyone who had good-natured torturers for brothers (and she had three, all older). On the whole, in the menagerie that was Ms. Rockower's third-grade class, I was the raucous howler monkey; Esther, a solitary, paranoid heron. Or, in other words, for a good while she couldn't stand me.

I, however, was infatuated by Esther straightaway. Every so often I would catch myself staring across the room at her—she'd avert her eyes from her work just long enough to shoot me a split-second look that nonetheless ran the emotional gamut: *Who, me? . . . Stop that! . . . Oh, God, I hope your bad behavior isn't an airborne contagion!!* And then she'd bury her head right back in the assignment. Even so, I was hell-bent on getting to know her, if for no other reason than I suspected, despite all our differences, that there was one thing we had in common: weirdness.

Our transition from diametrically opposed exotic little-girl animals to diametrically opposed exotic little-girl animals who were friends was predicated on one fateful confrontation during recess surrounding her pronunciation of my first name. For reasons neither of us can remember, Esther had had to call out my name during one of our class exercises. (Maybe we were doing a unit of math, and Ms. Rockower asked, "Who is the fourth person in the second row?" and Esther raised her hand and said, "Tara." Or maybe it was grammar: "Whose name has two syllables?" *Tara.* Or health: "Who thought it was very funny to stick pencils into her ears and wiggle them around, yelling, 'Look at my alien antennas!,' which caused both pink eraser tops to break off and get embedded deep inside her ears for months, then didn't tell her parents about it, even when they were completely panicked that she was going deaf, so they took her to the doctor's office, where said erasers had to be surgically removed?" *Tara*.)

No matter the exact circumstances, when Esther said my name in class that day, she did not pronounce it *Tara* (like *Sarah*), with the New York accent that I and everyone else around us had but, rather, *Tey-ra*. So the very first words I ever spoke to her were, "Eh! Why do you say my name funny!?" To which she nervously shot right back, "Um, maybe because during the summer, I went to Montana, where they talk different?" I spent the entire rest of recess walking a slow loop around the fenced-in giant square of bare asphalt that was the PS 133 recess yard, side by side with Esther.

"Montana!? What for?"

"My mom is in a . . . a group."

"What kinda group?"

"We just call it The Group."

"THE Group. Never heard of it."

"I don't know if it's really called THE Group. But that's what we call it."

"Oh . . . so, is it like camp?"

"No."

"Well, are there sports!?"

"No, it's not like that. I don't know . . . it's just a group."

"Oh, okay."

"Well, do you promise not to say anything?"

"Promise!"

"My brother told me, just this last time, that maybe, it's a . . . cult."

"Wow. I never met anybody in a cult before!"

"But I don't think we are going to go anymore now, though."

"Oh. Sorry."

"It's okay. So, what about you? Do you go anywhere, different, like, in the summer?"

"Wanna make another loop?"

And so it was that the tiniest demographic was then added to the PS 133 diaspora. There was the vast majority— multigenerational native New Yorkers of Italian or Irish heritage; the next-largest clique of recently immigrated Indian kids; tiny pockets of Asians, African Americans, and Latino kids; three Maltese sisters (this was Queens, after all); and, finally, Esther and I, the "my native New Yorker mom got herself into some seriously unique situation that has ping-ponged me back and forth from this small slice of working-class Queens to worlds unknown" kids.

By the end of fourth grade, Esther and I had made an Indy 500's worth of loops around the recess yard. The whole of my story was now clear to her, and she had revealed the whole of hers to me. Esther's mom grew up in an apartment above their family's delicatessen in New Jersey, worked the counter starting at age ten, saved her money, and put herself through Rutgers, earning a teaching degree. She then moved to California, where she met and married a man involved in a questionable, cultlike religious group that held yearly summertime retreats in rural Montana. They had four kids together and moved from California to Pennsylvania, but things soon deteriorated, so her mother came back to New York, this time to Bellerose, Queens, divorced, and was raising her children alone on a public school teacher's salary.

The particulars of our stories were as different as our personalities, but having "a story" was enough to bring us together, and by the start of Mrs. Miller's fifth-grade class, Esther and I were inseparable.

The effects of the skittish, goody-two-shoes, neat-as-a-pin girl becoming best friends with the scatterbrained, disheveled imp, were instantly apparent. I became a "morning monitor," a job that entailed tidying up the classroom before the start of the day, which I never would have been caught dead doing before, only because Esther was one, too. But a few days in I strong-armed her into using the teachers-only electric eraser-cleaning machine mounted to the wall of its own tiny hall closet, an offense she wouldn't have dreamed of before, and then accidentally let the door close behind us just as she turned it on. The cleaner screeched like an incoming subway train, and we screamed for what felt like ten minutes, trapped in the dark and hitting all sorts of buttons to try to shut it off, before some teacher yanked the door open and found us covered in chalk dust like two little powdered donuts. (Apparently one of those buttons we hit released the trash compartment.) It was Esther's first-ever trip to the principal's office.

Lunchtime had always been a hotbed of trouble for me, but having Esther by my side helped curb my troublemaking, most times. There were too many kids to all fit in the cafeteria at PS 133, so those of us who brought bagged lunch ate in the tiny auditorium on rows of metal folding chairs, leaving an empty one in between each kid to serve as a table split with your neighbor. It was a tight squeeze in a hot room, with a pungent swirl of bologna and curry. All of that would have been tolerable if it wasn't for Mrs. Golden.

A seventy-year-old, put-out-to-pasture former teacher assigned to oversee the "lunchroom," she demanded that we eat without talking in anything more than a hushed whisper. Really—some two hundred kids, desperate to get out to the recess yard, were prevented even from chit-chatting or laughing with any enthusiasm for a full fifteen minutes. If you spoke a single loud sentence, she would call you up to the front of the room and have you finish your lunch alone on a side bench, then bar you from going outside to the yard for the whole remaining recess.

I always sat with Esther, who spent ten of the fifteen minutes putting her index finger to her lips to remind me to keep my voice down. But once, after a fellow rebel got put in the clink for a giggle, I couldn't take it anymore. I stood up on my chair, let out a booming, pitch-perfect Tarzan howl, then jumped off and started running in circles around the auditorium with Mrs. Golden close at my heels. The entire room instantly went bat-shit. Kids were pounding their chairs into the linoleum, pumping their fists in the air, and screaming at the tops of their lungs like I had just hit a grand slam at Yankee Stadium. Then, of course, I was caught and dragged to the bench. When Mrs. Golden released everyone to the recess yard some five minutes later, Esther stopped at the door, turned, and came to sit next to me on the bench for the entire rest of recess. I could cry thinking about it now, but at the time I just gave her a love punch to the shoulder.

We still maintained some autonomy. There was no way I was joining the Color Guard, but I woo-hoo'ed for Esther when she marched by cradling the New York State flag propped in her weird, flag-holding, leather-belt contraption while "My Country, 'Tis of Thee" pumped out of the staticky auditorium speakers at any given ceremony. And Esther never once joined me on one of my fourth-floor excursions to asbestos-land, but always seemed genuinely concerned when she would ask me afterward if I had any trouble breathing.

As Esther had suspected, not long after we met, her mom stopped going to the Group, and so, by the start of fifth grade, her life of ricocheting between worlds was now over. The little bit of a Montana accent she had picked up soon faded and, with it, any additional questions from snooping classmates who might have wanted to hear her story. My social-strata-hopping life, however, was still in full swing, though I have no memory of wanting, or needing, to tell anyone other than Esther the details of it (at least not for many more years).

It's hard to imagine that no one at PS 133 ever questioned why, if it were a Wednesday after school, I would be playing handball with the rest of the kids, but every other Friday I would be getting into the stretch limousine Mark had sent to pick me up, but I truly can't recall a single real conversation about it back then (at least not anything more than, "Wow, is that thing here for you?" *Yup.*

Bye!). This had been my life since kindergarten, and by fifth grade the only change was that Esther often hopped into that limo with me.

When we jumped in with our high-tops, Table Talk cherry pies, bags of puffy Cheez Doodles, and quarter waters, we would sometimes find Mark inside: six feet and ten inches of pinstripe, sitting way down in the far end of the car, with his face buried in the *Times* and his knees, each the height of a four-year-old, slowly swinging out and in, then bumping at the center, then back out again, all in perfect rhythm as we drove. Meanwhile, Esther and I would play city-kid patty-cake, a superfast smacking of palms and laps and palms and laps, as we sang, "Went to the store to get a stick of butter, saw James Brown sitting in the gutter, took a piece of glass, shoved it up his ass, never seen a motherfucker run so fast, rockin' robin!" We dropped our voices to a whisper for the expletive finale, but even if we hadn't, Mark likely wouldn't have cared. To his credit, he never asked us to change.

We played many more rounds and more varieties of patty-cake—"Miss Lucy had a steamboat, the steamboat had a bell, toot-toot, Miss Lucy went to heaven, the steamboat went to hel/lo operator, please give me number nine, and if you disconnect me, I will chop off your behind/the 'frigerator there was a piece of glass, Miss Lucy sat upon it and broke her little ass/k me no more questions . . ."—in the Barn, or the Cottage, or on Adirondack chairs courtside while Mark practiced croquet. And at night we roller-skated around and around the screened-in porch of the Main House overlooking the lagoon pool, singing songs and showing off our choreographed moves while Mark smiled and swirled the cognac in his snifter, and Mom clapped along.

Esther and I would walk loops around his Bridgehampton estate, gabbing away, so far immersed in some imaginary fantasy-world game that the whole rest of the real world faded away, just the way we did on the asphalt recess yard at PS 133. And some odd Saturday nights with Mark we'd sit side by side at the swanky-white-tableclothed French restaurant on Main Street, just the way we did in the cramped auditorium lunchroom. In lieu of my typical lunch of a cold slice of Grandma's frittata (she sent it via the Grandpa Express all the way from Westport every week), I tended to go for the sole meunière, and instead of her usual bologna on white with mayo, Esther always, *always*, got the duck à l'orange. (Hey, Mrs. Fucking Golden, get a load of us now!)

By the end of fifth grade, we had likely spent as many days together in Bridgehampton as we did at Dad and Jackie's new place, as we did at my new house on 253rd Street, and at Esther's old one, on 237th. She knew all the Gregory's regulars and my rowdy Clancy family from Dad's house parties, and I got to know her older brothers—if you can call getting to know them being chased around and around the ten-square-foot patch of grass and asphalt of her backyard with brooms or paint rollers or whatever instruments of intimidation were on hand that day.

Beyond the average disdain older brothers have for their little sisters and her little friends, it likely didn't help our status with them that Esther regularly bragged about her duck à l'orange dinners when they were stuck at home having her mom's maximum-bang-for-the-buck vats of buttered noodles, or that Mark had once sent a limo to pick us up at Esther's house. Or, worse, that on one long weekend, when Mark expected bad traffic, he forewent the limo entirely and instead chartered a private plane.

My mother picked Esther and me up from PS 133 that day and drove us to the Marine Air Terminal at LaGuardia Airport in her beat-up Cutlass while doing her mascara in the rearview and smoking a cigarette. Sashaying out onto the tarmac—the three of us now doing our best impression of anyone with an upbringing different from ours—we met Mark, walking ahead in great strides, pinstripes like flagpoles now, carrying our bags headlong into the wind, his tie, her perm, and our backpack straps sailing backward as we went.

The pilot asked me if I wanted to take the copilot's seat. *Of course* I did, and, surprising all of us, he actually let me fly the thing or, to be realistic, steer it a few inches to the left for three seconds. In other words, at age ten, with Grandma and Broad Channel recently gone from my day-to-day life, when I was FLYING A PLANE over Shea Stadium, where my mother and grandfather had once sold hot dogs, and when I was sitting in front of the millionaire whose apartment my mom used to clean—THIS should have been the very moment my untethered spinning reached maximum velocity and I went spiraling off into the stratosphere, never to return. But I didn't, perhaps because also sitting in that plane was Esther. And she'd be there when we landed, and when we were back in school the following week, and the next weekend, whether we were at Dad's place or hers, the two of us spinning, together.

So while I may never have been truly tethered to a single reality, I was okay, in large part, because I was tethered to her.

10

Once a year, usually sometime after we finished dessert, I'd work up the nerve to ask Mark, "So, what was it like in your house, as a kid, growing up?" And once a year, he'd pause, look me in the eye, and say something along the lines of, "Now, I'd say that the tarte Tatin was quite good, possibly *very* good, but it likely would have benefited from somewhat less sugar. What are your thoughts?" And I'd take the hint . . . until the next year.

But after I had asked that same question a half dozen times in as many years, just once, following his standard pause and look, instead of steering me off course with a critique of the evening's pastry, Mark did give me an answer, of sorts. It felt like a broken-off bit of a much larger, much darker thought. A garbled little pair of words that just shot out of his subconscious like a pinball, ricocheted around his brain for a split second, then rocketed straight toward the drain: "Booze and grease ... just booze and grease."

He seemed as shocked to have said those words aloud as Mom and I were to have heard them. Afterward, for an emotionally very long but in reality very short moment, we all sat in silence shifting our gaze back and forth from the tablecloth to the curtains. Tablecloth. Curtains. Tablecloth. Curtains. Finally, mercifully, Mark started back in with his review of the soufflé.

I was eleven, too young to have a deep understanding of what summarizing the whole of your early family life and childhood home as "just booze and grease" might mean, but just old enough to know not to ask for an explanation. Which is maybe why, that same night, after his immediate diversion on dessert, he continued:

"My father had this old recliner, this tattered, grease-stained thing, and, after he'd come home from the mill, he'd pull it up to the television, right up there, an arm's length from the screen, and then he'd take a stack of Mallomars cookies and line them up on the armrests, six or so to a side, and during the commercial breaks he'd put two of them back to back, mash them together, ratchet open his jaw, and shove the whole mess in! Like this." And then he squashed an imaginary pair of the famous marshmallow-domed chocolate-covered treats between his fingers and rammed them two-knuckles-deep into his mouth.

Mom and I waited for him to burst out laughing before we joined in.

And that was it—those two tiny tidbits were the only things he ever told me directly about his childhood.

Over the years Mom did manage to glean a lot more details about Mark's past, but the fuller picture came together at such a glacial pace that she couldn't recall exactly when she learned what, let alone when she shared that information with me.

She knew that he grew up in a cramped two-bedroom apartment in a bleary mill town near Providence, Rhode Island, in what we would come to learn was the 1930s. (Among his many quirks, he never, ever, celebrated his birthday, nor revealed the date. Mom knew he was considerably older than she from the get-go, but it wasn't until she snuck a peek at his passport on a trip—a whole six years after they started dating—that she learned his actual age. He was twenty years her senior.)

He had just one sibling, a brother, who was a couple of years younger and exactly one inch shorter, a measly 6'9". After the age of twelve neither of them had a single pair of pants that went much past their mid-calves.

Mark's grandfather, father, and uncles hadn't gone be-yond high school, and all worked at the town paper mill, but Mark went to Providence College on a basketball scholarship. He wasn't a very good high school player, but, considering his extraordinary height, the college coaches took him on anyway, presuming they could teach him. They couldn't. He was a self-described "god-awful, bench-warming ignoramus" for all four years.

Right after graduation he got married and became a fireman. But by his mid-twenties he left the fire depart-ment to take a job as the mail boy at the New England Bell Telephone Company in the hope of climbing the cor-porate ladder. He did.

After that he got a job as the branch manager of a local bank and soon rose to managing several branches. And then he got a management position at IBM. He moved to West-chester, New York, where the company's headquarters were located, and, once there, he and his wife had two daughters.

Mark left IBM several years later when he was offered the job of executive vice president of Citibank. Shortly afterward, somewhere around his fiftieth birthday, he got divorced. Not long after that, he got laid off. And so, he put it all on the line and decided to start his own man-agement consulting company. He convinced two Citibank colleagues to join him: a female executive signed on as his vice president and Sally, the mutual friend of my parents from Broad Channel, became his secretary. And that was the whole operation. By the time Mom became his short-lived third employee just a few years later, his consulting services were being sought after by Fortune 50 companies, and Mark had officially catapulted from "booze and grease" to Bridgehampton.

At age eleven, I still wouldn't have described Mark as a "new money" guy with "old money" taste, but I definitely could have told you that he was very different from my parents and grandparents. And I might have been able to articulate that difference with a side-by-side comparison of their hobbies, or music preferences, but mostly by how they would have cursed somebody out. Dad's arsenal of insults ranged from the almost quaint—ya piece a' work, ya jerk, ya mope—to a terrible, exhaustive collection of racial, ethnic, and religion-based epithets, the only possible consolation to this being that most of them were so antiquated that it would be years before I had any idea that he wasn't just making weird sounds when he got angry: Nip, Yid, Wop, Zip, Mick. Huh?

Grandpa just didn't have it in him to yell at real people in real life, but on occasion he'd hurl a "fathead" or "banana-head" at the ball game on TV. Grandma, meanwhile, addressed the people she loved most in this world as "devil semen" (*sfacimm*), even if she was just calling you home for dinner, but she did reserve a few choice phrases for people who actually wronged her: e.g., *Fanabla, puttana!* (Go to hell, whore!).

I don't mean to leave Mom out, but, well, suffice to say, she got mugged on the subway once—a group of girls pinned her down on the floor of the train, tore open her blouse, and ripped the necklace right off her neck—and the worst she could muster when describing them was "not nice people."

But, for Mark, fatheads, *sfacimms*, mopes, and worse, were imbeciles, dimwits, or morons. So he not only walked the old-money walk—art, antiques, croquet—he talked the old-money talk. And when you put the two together, it might have appeared he was affecting high society in a Hollywood movie–style attempt to slip undetected into some elite social scene and climb the ranks, if it weren't for one thing: us. And by us, I don't just mean Mom and me; I mean all thirty-two members of my Riccobono family. Because by the time I was eleven, it was clear that Mark didn't have, or want, an upper-crust circle of friends. In fact, by then, Mark was just Riccobono number thirty-three, and, like the rest of us, his family became his friends.

I'm crawling top speed along the front lawn in Bridge-hampton through a thirty-foot tunnel maze of banquet tables. Above me, the catering staff are setting out triangular infantries of wineglasses, short stacks of real porcelain cheese plates, salad plates, and dinner plates, and row after row of Mark's solid silver antique cutlery—every few feet I accidentally bump a table leg, setting off a symphony of rattling dinnerware, before poking my head out and yelling to the nearest caterer, "Sorry! I'll slow it up!"

Above the tables and the caterers and the trees and the clouds, smashed in the backs of tiny prop planes, are my Uncle Vinny, Aunt Jeanie, and their six kids. In another are my Uncle Jimmy, Aunt Marlene, and their three sons. In yet another are my Aunt Lucille, Uncle Ed, and their two kids. This entire little fleet is about to drop bombs of loud Brooklyn-bred Italians onto the tarmac of East Hampton Airport.

And that's not even half of them. The remaining platoons—Aunt Joanne, Uncle Tony, and their three kids; Uncle Sal, his two sons, and his girlfriend, Patty; Great-uncle Jerry and his boyfriend, John; and Grandma and Grandpa—are all coming via limousine. In other words, it's an all-out air and ground assault, the lot of them just seconds from making landfall, where they will swell into a small army and send wafts of garlicky air out into the nostrils of old WASPs who'll either drop dead mid-swing at the sixteenth hole or be struck with a sudden urge for spaghetti.

This is the fourth inaugural attack of The Riccobonos on The Republic of Bridgehampton, a.k.a. the annual summer party Mark throws for our family. He first broached the idea at one of our basement parties on 251st Street, years earlier, crammed next to Aunt Lucille and Uncle Tony in our tiny Queens basement, eating a meatball on a metal folding chair. I remember him saying two things: 1) having attended all of our parties, he wanted to return the favor—Mark was by then a regular at my uncles' Jets tailgates and could be seen, any given Sunday, standing there in his Burberry coat at 8:00 a.m., drinking Delamain cognac out of a plastic cup. And he never missed a Christmas Eve, New Year's Day, Thanksgiving, or Easter at Grandma's, who also refused any of the more traditional offers of thanks; i.e., food or money: "Can you bring something? What you gonna bring? Some junk shit you buy at the store? I cook, from scratch! *Stunad!*" Or: "What, you want me to take your money, like I'm some *puttana* on the street?! I cook! I pay! Don't ask again! *Che cazzo!*" And, 2) if we accepted the invitation, there was one hitch: he insisted on supplying all transportation, to avoid what he dubbed a "Riccobono rendezvous." Everyone shot him the eye, knowing some ball busting was coming, and then he impersonated one of my uncles, in a mock-conversation with another of my uncles, organizing a family get-together, *"Okay, I got it all figured—Jimmy picks up Vinny, who picks up Tony, who picked up Lu, who picks up Joanne, who picked up Cah-mella, who picks up Patty, who tells Sal to pick up Danny, to pick up Peter, to pick up Jeannie—*and maybe, just maybe, after you all have crisscrossed the tristate area several hundred times and burned a tanker's worth of gasoline, you manage to show up for dinner." Everybody cracked up, and then Grandma coined a term of her own, a nickname for Mark, "Okay, your party, your way, *Mastagotz*" (something akin to Mr. Big Dick, which quickly became what everyone in our family, from the age of sixteen up, also called him).

Mark's party, Mark's way, is a French-country-picnic-themed affair, complete with a spare-tire-size wheel of Gruyère cheese, platter after platter of cod *en papillote* and chicken paillard, a clam bar, and endless cases of Beaujolais. There are a half dozen white-tablecloth-covered round tables with matching white wooden chairs, each table topped with candles encased in vintage glass hurricane lamps and centerpiece vases of Mom's wildflower arrangements. And the whole spread is set out under the enormous canopy of the sole, stunning, ancient elm tree that sits in the middle of the vast front lawn, its leaves fluttering about with each gust of salty beach air. It's nothing short of magical, a Great Gatsby—caliber bash, but even better because all the blue-blooded schmucks have been replaced by Brooklyn Italians.

I'm midway through my umpteenth race-car crawl under the now fully set banquet tables, when my ears perk up. The pristine country quiet is breached by the slow-building grumblings of arriving Riccobonos—a gradual swell that starts with the closing of car doors and the trampling of feet and then suddenly erupts when the first head pokes past the driveway gate. "HELLOOO! Yoo-hoo! We made it!" "WHOA! Will ya getta load of this!! Looks even better than last year!" "Eh, *Mastagotz!* Where are ya? We're here!!" I shimmy out from under the table and book it in their direction.

My aunts and uncles plant kisses on my forehead as they pass, and I gather up my cousins: "Come on, hurry up! Go get your suits on so we can go in the pool before they make us stop to eat!" Mom drops her basket of just-cut flowers and comes running over to give and get hugs. "Hiya, Mel! The place looks beautiful, as always." Then Mark saunters over from the croquet court, mallet in hand: "All right, can we quit it already? Hugging each other like you've just returned from years in Siberia? The first match of the day starts now—all interested parties, dump the bags, grab cocktails, and meet me courtside!"

Uncle Vinny pipes up: "You're going down, *Mastagotz!* If not now, then later—this year we're making you play Wiffle ball!"

"Ah, yes, Wiffle ball—esteemed sport of morons everywhere. Not a chance."

"Every year, same shit with you. I bet you don't like it 'cause you suck at it."

"Highly likely. And I'm starting to think I 'suck' at croquet, too, seeing as how your brother Sal has been kicking my ass these last few years!"

"As a kid he was always the best stickball player on the block, but croquet—who knew!?"

They were about to head off for the court, when Mom yelled out, "Eh! Vin! Mommy and Daddy aren't here yet!?"

There was a good ten minutes' worth of panic before we heard the limo pull up. Grandma and Grandpa had spent the last half hour stuck behind future secretary of state, then chairman of the Joint Chiefs of Staff, four-star U.S. army general Colin Powell's security brigade, bringing him to his country house, right across the street from Mark's.

Even before the toe of her shoe poked out from the limo door, Grandma's curse words hit the air and traveled mach-speed into each and every one of our ears, *"Fahngool! Che cazzo! Minchia!* Traffic!" and no matter where we were—in the pool, by the croquet court, piling up a plate of chicken paillard—everybody stopped dead, then rushed toward her and got into formation. We lined up one by one, some forty of us—dripping wet, mallet in hand, shoving that last bite of Gruyère into our mouths—in this long, snaking line on Mark's manicured front lawn, and approached to kiss her. (She never, ever kissed you back; she just offered up a cheek.) Meanwhile Grandpa, wearing his standard perma-grin, stood at her side, giving us loving pats on the head, pokes in the belly, and bear hugs, in between still trying to calm her down, "Okay, Rose. It's over now. We are here. Let's have a nice time!" Which, of course, didn't work.

"Okay Rose?! Okay Rose?! I'll give you *'Okay Rose!'* Fahn-gool!"*

After countless games of croquet, one human pyramid made up of all seventeen of my cousins in the lagoon pool (oldest on the bottom, next row on their shoulders, and so on and so on), and one Wiffle-ball tournament (Mark came in for one at-bat, running the bases despite being struck out by Uncle Vinny, who laughed so hard, he actually fell to the grass and rolled around), we had dinner. And then the party moved onto the screened porch for dessert.

Mark had special-ordered these chocolate truffle cakes, so rich they were sliced superthin, which my cousin Danny interpreted as the work of a skimpy caterer, so, after everyone else had had a piece, he kept going back for more. Only after he had been at it a good while did someone finally notice, "Eh! *Gavone!* Don't you think that's enough?!" Then they counted—he had eaten thirteen slices. He was twelve.

We saved one of the most time-honored Riccobono traditions for last: arm-wrestling. The first few matches were goofs—Uncle Sal (down to his tight white crewneck undershirt, a ringer for the Fonz) versus Great-uncle Jelly (as gay as ever in his captain's hat, button-down shirt open to the sternum, and ascot). Then Uncle Sal versus Grandma, who instantly snatched the nearby hands of two of my little cousins, stacked them behind her own, and screamed, "Push! Push, you little *sfacimms!* Grandma don't lose—even if she has to cheat!" After that the real battles began, twenty-minute all-out dogfights, everybody hooting and pounding the tables, as one by one, Uncle Sal took down Grandpa, then my oldest cousins, Anthony and Mike. And at that we called it a night; the sweat-soaked arm wrestlers, the hoarse-throated onlookers, and all their sleepwalking children headed back out to the driveway and pulled away as Mom and I stood there waving good-bye.

When we walked back, we found Mark still sitting on the porch, looking out at the night sky, swirling the cognac in his snifter, and knocking his knees as always. Mom came up behind him, wrapped her arms around his shoulders, and kissed his left cheek, and I scooted around to give him a rare peck on the right. And then he took her hand, and mine, and we stayed that way, staring up at the moon—neither the three of us, nor the thirty of the departing Riccobonos, having the slightest inkling that this year's Bridgehampton party would be the last.

11

I'm staring up into the sky again, but this time it's mid-morning, in Brooklyn. I'm ten years old, and I'm standing side by side with my grandpa on the shoulder of the Belt Parkway. I have no idea why we're here or what we're looking for, but I'm copying him anyway, feet glued to the grass, head tilted straight back, hawk-eyeing the *nothing* above a giant chain-link fence that surrounds a park that abuts the parkway shoulder. We wait. And we wait. And wait. Between the roar of the cars whizzing by our backs and the zero warning he gave two minutes earlier before pulling off the highway, throwing the car into park, hopping out, trotting around to my side, swinging open the door, and saying nothing beyond, "Come on, Shrimpy!" I am as scared as I am confused. But I went. So here I am.

Earlier this morning, when Mom told me I'd be going with Grandpa to his office today—I had the day off from school, and she had to work—I was thrilled. Having Grandpa stay at our house during the week these last six months has brought two distinct perks: the first is that, at night, when Mom hollers into our room, "Eh, Da! I know the game isn't over, but you gotta shut it off! It's late! Tara has to go to sleep now!" he doesn't. He tiptoes over to the TV, raises his hand up to the knob, then turns back to me, winks, and mutes the volume instead. And we stay up, my legs dangling off the top bunk right above him, the both of us miming victory screams and doing exaggerated soundless boos at the Mets for a good hour past bedtime.

And the second perk is getting to go with Grandpa to his job at the most wonderful Metropolitan Life Insurance Company branch of Bay Ridge, Brooklyn. I've gone twice before, and both times it went something like this:

We head off in the morning in "Chucky," Grandpa's beaten-up-to-within-an-inch-of-its-life Buick LeSabre, which I've nicknamed based on the sound the engine makes when he starts it—*chuck, chuck, chuck, chuck, chuck, chuck, chuck, chuck, chuck, Vroom!!* Traveling in Chucky was an experience in itself. The old girl was mostly a sun-worn maroon color, with two exceptions: the first being the half dozen rust-pancake splotches on the hood and trunk; the second being the one door panel Grandpa had replaced, which was gray. Inside were cloth seats that were torn at the seams and a felt ceiling that had started to droop, leaving these giant billowed sections of fabric that very literally sat on your head. The backseat was occupied entirely by a row of overflowing cardboard boxes (his "work papers") topped with trash: empty fast-food containers, wrappers, napkins, etc. And Grandpa kept receipts and business cards, hundreds of them lumped together, as thick as a novel, attached with rubber bands to the driver's side visor—the whole mess dangling a hair above his eyes as he drove. Every inch of that car was cluttered, even the ashtray, where he kept a bottle of Old Spice on top of a mound of loose change. And, because he refused to drive any less than eight million miles an hour, as soon as we hit the highway, the two of us were instantly in the eye of this tornado of junk—getting thwacked in the head by the odd foam cup that took flight from the backseat, swatting away rogue receipts that had come loose from his visor, peeling off cellophane candy wrappers that suddenly pasted themselves to our cheeks. He grinned away all the while, seemingly oblivious to the whirlwind of crap obstructing his vision, crisscrossing lanes with one hand

and trying to tune in the sportscast on 1010 WINS with the other. Until we arrived.

I spent the first several hours in the office in total bliss—i.e., eating M&M's while pounding out gibberish on a typewriter that had been set out on a special desk just for me. Then we took a trip to the Brownsville and East New York housing projects to visit Grandpa's clients, who gave me even more candy and let me pet their cats. Finally, we made an after-work stop at a Bay Ridge public park, where Grandpa and a half dozen other elderly Italian men met up regularly to kick dirt at one another and curse the heavens, a.k.a., play *bocce.* And at that, we called it a day—perfect.

But this one, trip number three, was different. It started the very same way as the first two, except at some point after we took off in Chucky from our house on 253rd Street but before we arrived at Grandpa's office, he pulled off the parkway and onto the shoulder.

After standing at the foot of that fence for what seemed like forever—side by side, staring up, glued still, looking more and more like the lone constituents of some wing-nut cult who believed their messiah was set to emerge from a cloud over the Belt Parkway in Brooklyn—finally I saw something. It was tiny and yellow and came hurtling toward us. It landed on the grass and bounced. And only then did I look down, my eyes scanning the grass in larger and larger concentric circles, growing wider with disbelief. There were tennis balls, everywhere. A minefield of tennis balls!

In a wink Grandpa dropped down onto his hands and knees, stretched out his shirt, and started scooping them up. I did the same and then followed him back to Chucky, parked behind us. He threw open the trunk, and inside there must have been a hundred used tennis balls! We dumped ours on top and got back into the car.

At this point, I was so excited because he was so excited, and he was so excited because he'd just let me in on this secret tennis ball free-for-all—we alone were reaping the rewards of some Parks Department architect's error, it seemed, a grave miscalculation of how high a given tennis ball hit at such-and-such miles an hour could go, with the wind gusts in a particular direction, and the phase of the moon on a chosen Wednesday in autumn in Brooklyn. And their underestimation was to our great benefit.

At seventy-five, my grandpa had been selling life insurance policies for over twenty years—a job that entailed being there when people assigned themselves a retail value while simultaneously imagining their own deaths. In other words, his job was not most people's idea of a good time, but the way he smiled all day long at work, and the way his clients smiled back at him, you'd have thought Bruno "Ricky" Riccobono made his living as a professional provider of free ice cream cones.

He was one of the top salesmen at MetLife for two reasons: 1) he was the first agent at his branch to see poorer people as potential customers, and, having gone door to door in the Brooklyn projects to build his business in the late 1970s, by 1990 he had a large and loyal pool of clients; 2) he wholeheartedly believed in the concept of life insurance: being ready for the worst but hoping for the best (which in this case is just the worst, plus money). He was the happiest guy I knew and nothing if not prepared. To this day I have no idea when or how Grandpa figured out that there were all these tennis balls on this particular shoulder of the Belt Parkway. And it's not that he, or I, or anyone we knew, played tennis. But had that ever changed, we'd have been ready.

Unfortunately, what ultimately claimed the life of Mark's all-out Bridgehampton summer parties was that he didn't share Grandpa's philosophy—it would be another decade before I knew it, but it would seem that Mark's version was more like "be ready for the best. The end." What I'm saying is, while Mark's Lincoln Continental had a mighty big trunk, there was nary more than a single shirtful of found tennis balls thumping around inside at any one time. Mark had no "insurance policy," no savings, and when you're not prepared and the worst comes, it's just that, the worst. There's no consolation prize.

Given how careful Grandpa was with his money, how much he constantly impressed that diligence upon us, and how much he loved Mark, it would have killed him to know that one day Mark would face hard times because no one had impressed those same lessons upon him. But, sadder still, a heart attack did the deed long before that day would come. Grandpa died in 1991, at seventy-six, about six months after our famed tennis-ball-harvesting on the Belt Parkway.

Mom and I weren't there, but he was at our house on 253rd Street that night with Grandma—they were headed to Atlantic City in Jersey for a weekend vacation and had decided to break up the driving from Connecticut with a stay in Queens.

The funeral was held two weeks after my eleventh birthday, and though I had known Mark for eight years by then, it was the first time I had ever seen him cry.

I can remember only one thing about my own mourning: a month after Grandpa died, Mom told me she thought it might be good for me to get a new single bed. I refused to let her take away *our* bunk for a full year.

Grandma was wrecked, of course, but after a while she decided to go through those hundreds of receipts from Grandpa's visor, and, having found a good dozen or so from Nathan's in Coney Island, her sadness turned to rage. "Three hot dogs!! THREE!!! With his cholesterol what it was! No wonder he croaked! Had I known, I'd have wrung his neck myself. *Fahngool!*"

Consequently, having a lot more free time and without Grandpa to keep her in check, Grandma became more and more obsessed with hitting the slots in Atlantic City. Mom and I started taking her once a month, and pretty soon she was dropping so much cash that our hotel room and all our meals were comped. She talked constantly about her beloved "comps," the complimentary offerings casinos afforded the biggest losers, and at eleven I had no trouble subscribing to her logic. Spend half your life savings for a free trip to the shoddy Golden Nugget breakfast buffet and a Betamax VCR? Sounds fair to me.

The king of all the comps was what Grandma referred to exclusively as "the Basket." It was your standard gift basket, a half dozen unrecognizably branded chocolate-covered treats, nut mixes, and maybe an apple or two, all propped up on fake shredded grass. And once Grandma hit "whale" status in money lost, it was supposed to be in our room whenever we arrived. But it never was. That room could have been on fire, and she wouldn't have noticed, but if "the Basket" wasn't there, she would flip her shit. "*Che cazzo!* Where's the Basket?! You call and tell them to bring it up now!!"

The very first time she asked me to make that call, I was embarrassed and looking for a way out, so I asked, "Grams, why don't you just do it?"

"*Minchia!* Why, she asks!? Why?! Because I don't talk nice, that's why! But you do! You call and you use the nice words, like *Mastagotz* taught you." I knew exactly what she meant, but I hadn't known that she, or anyone in my family, had noticed that I sounded different when I spoke with Mark, that I used "nice words," or that I dropped my accent as low as it could go. In fact, I don't think *I* was even aware that I did it, until right then.

If I was indeed a little supergirl, able to jump social strata in a single bound, this was the first time I had been asked to hop into the phone booth, swap outfits, and use my powers in my civilian life. But, of course, I did as Grandma asked: "Good afternoon, I'm calling from Room 203. I don't mean to be a bother, but it seems we're missing our complimentary gift basket. Would it be possible for someone to send it up?" *You bettah get right on it—or my grandma's gonna come down there and rip your fucking heart out!* "Thank you ever so much!"

That was that—I broke superhero protocol for twelve bucks' worth of half-decent snacks. And it felt great.

As it turned out, this year of rule-breaking and risk-taking—by the Parkway with Grandpa, at the casino with Grandma—was just the tip of the iceberg for me. The real risk-taking watershed was still to come, and when it did, I would no longer be a little kid. I would be a preteen Viking girl, forged in the asphalt "fields" of the Catholic Youth Organization sports league alongside a dozen other ponytailed badasses, then tested in the concrete recess battle yard of Middle School 172.

12

We're down by one, two outs, no men on, no men anywhere: this is bantam-division softball, and we're eleven-year-old girls. I am in the dugout, wringing my hands, nervous as hell, watching as our best player, Michelle, approaches the plate, helicoptering the bat over her head as if this is the World Series and not just another Catholic Youth Organization game on a garbage-strewn blacktop in Queens.

We aren't the Bulldogs or Tomcats or even the Lady Bulldogs or Lady Tomcats. We are St. Gregory the Great. The teams in the CYO didn't have any nicknames or mascots; they were just named after their church. The more colorful ones in our division in the early '90s were Our Lady of the Blessed Sacrament, Our Lady of Perpetual Help, and St. Pancras, named for the fourteen-year-old martyr beheaded by Emperor Diocletian. And on this day, we are playing our rivals, the Immaculate Conception Youth Program. In other words, it was us versus the greatest miracle of all time.

This being New York City, not every team in our league had access to cars, and any given Saturday you'd see two girls tag-teaming a duffel bag of equipment the size of a sixth-grader up the subway stairs, sweat-soaked before the game even began. Most others crisscrossed the borough in a caravan of tiny sedans smashed full of girls, a floral arrangement of arms, bats, and banners poking out the windows as they flew down the Van Wyck Expressway. The league represented what seemed like every neighborhood and ethnic group, regardless of creed. I remember a Muslim girl who wore a ball cap over her hijab and a long-sleeve shirt under her St. Something-or-Other jersey.

My team, St. Greg's, from Bellerose, was made up of Clancys, Kellys, and Donaghues, with a sprinkling of Colacis and Nascimentos, too. Most of our fathers were cops or construction workers, but come Saturday, they became coaches and cheerleaders, sipping beers concealed in those refillable, bendy straw, sports bottles between shouts of "Eh! You gonna take a swing sometime this year?" and "Atta girl! Drive that ball right through her!"

Michelle scans the handful of dads behind the backstop, gets a couple of "you can do it" fist pumps, then stamps into the box, curls her lip, and smacks the first pitch into left field for a double. As the pitcher winds up again facing the next batter, she sprints off to steal third. After just two strides the catcher eyes her and rockets the ball to the third baseman. It should be over. But then Michelle does something that no one on our team, or the other team, has ever done (or seen) before. She slides. On asphalt.

Time stops, the clouds freeze in the sky, the whole planet comes to a grinding halt, and then every single person in sight gasps, in unison, *"Huhhhh!!!"*

The third baseman is just standing there looking down at Michelle, ball in her glove, still way up high, frozen in shock. At long last, the gobsmacked umpire goes, "Uh . . . ? Safe?!" And—*ka-bam*—all the girls on my team go off the rails! We let out primal screams, "RAHHH!!!!" I fling myself up onto the dugout fence, my fingers through the chain-link, and I shake it and shake it, roaring at the top of my lungs.

Meanwhile, one by one, the girls of the Immaculate Conception start throwing their gloves to the ground and join the chorus of their mothers screaming, "You can't do that!!" Some dad yells, "Disgusting! Who the hell tells a young girl to slide on concrete?!" Somebody's grandma even screamed, "God will punish you for this!" Our tough-ass dads, for the first time ever, are shocked silent.

Finally the umpire and coaches meet out on the mound, and they are out there for what feels like forever until, ultimately, they all agreed—as it turned out, there was no written rule against sliding on asphalt, so the call stayed. The move, however, was officially deemed "a pretty stupid idea," and they gave us all some shit about never doing it again. Little did they know, it was too late—right then and there, we had rechristened ourselves Our Lady of Perpetual Scrapes. The revolution had begun.

As it turns out, sliding on asphalt doesn't really involve much sliding. Done perfectly, you travel a couple of inches, tearing a hole in your pants as you go and skidding to a stop with only the first layer of skin removed. Done wrong, you either need a dozen stitches or you hit the ground with such impact that you instantly stop dead, then crab-walk the rest of the way in shame. In either case, you're left with a bruise the size of Connecticut, but if you are an eleven-year-old girl in the CYO bantam division of 1991 playing on asphalt, you succeed time after time, because no one expects you to care enough to try—99 percent of the time, they never even see you coming! And I know because, following this game, damn near every girl on my team would go on to do it.

My first time was a few games later. I was rounding toward home, head down in a full-tilt sprint, just a few steps away from the plate, when I looked up, just in time to see the throw come in. The catcher was ready to tag me, so I did a swan dive right up and over her. And then I came down, headfirst.

My lights went out for a few seconds, and then—*blink, blink, blink*—Dad is standing above me, waving two fingers in front of my face, steam coming out of his ears. The first thing I say is, "So!?" And he says, "I don't think it's a concussion." And I say, "No! Not that!" He doesn't get it. I say again, "SO???" And his head keeps shaking, but it goes from signaling confusion to you-gotta-be-kiddin'-me astonishment. "OH, FOR PETE's—Safe! You were safe, ya nut!"

We girls of the Catholic Youth Organization fast-pitch softball league played on "hardtop" for no other reason than that we were girls. Even the nine-year-old boys' baseball teams—whose pitchers' 45-mph fastballs barely matched ours—outranked us and were given dominion over the city's few dirt fields. And we were relegated to New York's least desirable playing fields—and the most dangerous. This fateful Sliding on Asphalt year, we were eleven—little but not too little to know that this was seriously fucked up. And so we were easily possessed by the spirit of the desperation play: to win, to shock the grandmas and piss off the moms, to impress the dads, to prove that we could play as hard as the boys, but more than anything to prove that we could play as hard as one another.

As it turned out, the timing couldn't have been better. Just a few months after the end of that softball season, I started middle school, where knowing how to play hard and being prepared to face-plant onto asphalt was not an option but a necessity.

I'm looking down, minding my own business, kicking up pebbles in the middle of the gray concrete yard at Middle School 172, when a pair of running, screaming girls clip my arm. My eyes shoot up—these girls are not so much holding hands as damn near ripping each other's arms out of the sockets as they pass, chanting, "FIGHT! FIGHT! FIGHT!" I bounce onto my tiptoes to watch as they clothesline their way through the crowd in front of me and then jump, arms wide, into a huddle of kids I hadn't noticed before in a far corner of the yard. *"FIGHT! FIGHT! FIGHT!"* I spin around. The other three-hundred-some-odd sixth-graders playing in the yard behind me are now just a sea of planted feet and perked heads, dead still for a solid second, until—*whoosh!*—they stampede.

Cartons of cafeteria milk and candy wrappers blow back behind them, and basketballs and handballs bounce away on their own, as the entire tidal wave speeds straight in my direction, hurtling a growing minefield of chucked backpacks in its wake. *Oh, shit.* I backpedal away, then pivot and dip into a full sprint, heading for the knee-high concrete wall that anchors the twenty-foot chain-link fence along the perimeter of the yard. Another dozen kids have the same idea, and some perch on the concrete base, necks straining to see what's going on, while others scale the fence sideways, Spider-Man style, for an even better view.

The fight chant is peppered with screams of pain and a chorus of "Fuck you, bitch!" The heads of the massive circle of kids surrounding whoever's fighting windshield-wipe at mach speed, letting out louder and louder "oohs" and "aahs." I can't see anything until the swarm moves all the way to the fence, and then, just ten feet ahead of me, I see a girl lift the loose bottom end of the chain-link with her left hand and shove the head of another girl underneath it with her right. The standing girl pummels the body of the trapped-by-the-neck, nearly guillotined girl for as long as it takes the team of security guards, blowing their whistles and spreading the crowd with their batons, to push through and wrestle the aggressor to the ground.

It is my first day of sixth grade, my first year in middle school. I am eleven. So are those two girls.

There are about a thousand kids in MS 172, from the sixth to the eighth grade, but only half of them actually want to beat the shit out of one another. The other half just look like they do.

Our school's population contains at least one member of nearly every ethnic and religious group, native New Yorkers and recent immigrants alike, with no clear majority, though the Indian kids were the newest addition to the neighborhood. Their official arrival was marked by one of my favorite, distinctly New York City phenomena—the sudden appearance of their favorite snack food, alongside that of the next most recent immigrant group, in the Key Food specialty section.

I still remember shopping there with Grandma, back when I was in PS 133, when she spotted a box of jelly candies, technically Bhagat's Keshar Badam Halwa with Saffron, sitting next to the red tin cubes of Lazzaroni Amaretti di Saronno cookies. Grandma flagged down a lady in a sari. "Eh! These any good?" The lady nodded and smiled. "They are sweet."

"I like sweet," Grandma said, throwing a box into her cart.

"And these?" the woman in the sari asked, pointing at the tin boxes of cookies.

"Sweet," Grandma said. So the lady took a box of those, as well—two people from very different parts of the world, brought together, if only for a second, by an exchange of their ridiculously cumbersomely named desserts.

Some of the kids who go to MS 172 live in apartments above the storefronts on Jamaica Avenue, or the Glen Oaks town houses. Others have small houses in Bellerose or big ones in Hollis Hills. But none of that means much, because it is Queens in 1991. And so, no matter where you're from, how much money you've got, or whether you are more inclined to guillotine a girl with a chain-link fence or join the chess club, everyone worships at the same altar: hip-hop.

Freckle-faced white girls wear their hair in slick-backed ponytails. Baby-faced black boys peek out from low-brimmed leather baseball caps. Chinese girls rock brown lip liner. Israeli boys wear Hilfiger button-downs, their gold-charm Hebrew *Chai* symbols hanging in the vee of their still-hairless chests (substitute Irish four-leaf clovers, Italian horns, Boricua flags, Jordan jersey number 23's, Yankee pendants, ankhs, Ganeshas, Shivas, or *Om*s, accordingly). And everybody has at least one Hugo Boss sweatshirt—if not a real one, then a pretty good knockoff.

Nadira Gonzales, president of the student council and lead in this year's production of *Oliver!*, otherwise channels Mary J. Blige in a Nautica puffy jacket, door-knocker earrings, and Timberlands. And Renita Samuel, who just a year ago, back when we were in PS 133, wore saris or matching polka-dotted short sets and jellies, now sports Knicks jerseys, Jordans, and a feigned bad-bitch scowl. For these most recent Indian immigrant kids, the transformation from acclimating American elementary school students to LL Cool J–wannabe middle school students especially stood out: some, like Renita, nailed the look; others, like Amul, missed by an inch that might as well have been a mile—he came to his first day of sixth grade at MS 172 in jeans, a T-shirt, and a pair of piss-poor rip-off Nikes called Shooters, and he took hell for it.

As always, Dad took me sneaker shopping on Liberty Avenue in Richmond Hill before school started that year. He had just moved into his first proper house barely across the Nassau border in the suburban town of Valley Stream, marking the first time in his forty-one years he had lived outside of Queens County. He didn't know of a sneaker store in his new neighborhood, but even if he had, Dad was of the old-school New York variety that would drive clear across the city to avoid spending money at a place where he didn't know the owner's name, his or her kids' names, and how they took their coffee.

We stopped at Marlowe Jewelers first. We weren't in the market for jewelry that day, or most other days we went shopping on Liberty, but Dad was close friends with everybody who worked there—"Slim," "Cha-tze," Dennis—so, from as early an age as I can remember, we always popped by with coffee and donuts and spent a half hour shooting the shit.

I so loved going to Marlowe's with Dad that it's preserved in my memory as clearly as Grandma's kitchen on

251st Street, or our old little house in Broad Channel: the way the glass jewelry cases and motorized, spinning watch displays rattled every time the elevated A train passed overhead; the deep, terrifying barks of Kiki (their German shepherd guard dog) whenever a new face came through the shop door; the nail-studded bat mounted on the back wall (if it weren't for the LOUISVILLE SLUGGER logo, you'd swear that thing had survived the gladiator contests of the Middle Ages).

While Dad chitchatted with Slim and Dennis, I eyed the nameplate necklaces that half the girls in my sixth-grade class already had. I waited until we were about to leave to point them out to Dad. "Christmas?" I asked. I got a "Maybe," which was more than enough to light me up.

We shot a wave to Manny in the window of G & R Electronics as we passed by, and then we headed into the sneakers shop. Dad got straight to talking baseball with Myron, the owner, while I tried on pair after pair—Ewings, Nike Air Maxes, Bo Jacksons, Filas, all-white high-top Reeboks with gum soles—staring at my feet in the little floor mirror for five, ten minutes apiece, then walking circles around the benches in the middle of the shop, then sidling back to the mirror, until Dad couldn't take it anymore, "For the love of God, Scooter, just pick a damn pair! I don't get you kids and this sneaker shit these days." I went for the Reeboks, then pushed my luck. "Eh, Da, any chance we could check if Sukon's got the Shockwaves in before we go home? They said they were coming this month."

For all my wannabe-tough-city-kid style, I was only eleven—young enough to still be collecting G.I. Joe figurines, old enough to know, after seeing that fight on my first day of sixth grade, that I needed to make more friends at MS 172 if I wanted to avoid getting my ass kicked.

Lynette Solina wore the unique dual crown of prettiest and toughest girl in our whole sixth-grade class. And even though Esther and I still faced no competition for the "weirdest" label, midway through that year Lynette had turned our best-friend twosome into a threesome.

We sat together every day in the cafeteria and spent the entire first week of our friendship seeing who could keep a Cry Baby Extra Sour Gumball in her mouth the longest, and talking about Jimmy, Lynette's infamous first boyfriend from earlier that year. Jimmy was technically in seventh grade, a year ahead of us, but he had been left back so many times, he was fourteen (to our eleven). And for reasons no one understood, one day he walked into the yard with a BB gun and shot two kids in their asses.

We knew that the recess fight riots at 172 were a daily thing, but this episode still took the cake. And even though Jimmy was immediately expelled, we panicked that he might come back anyway. So we hypothesized on what Lynette should do if he did. Esther, true to form, i.e., petrified, ventured: "You didn't ever really break up with him, Lynette, right? Maybe you can't! It might make him mad! What if he comes after you!? You're stuck!"

"Yeah! You probably have to marry him now, just so he doesn't shoot you, too!" I chimed in, trying to be funny and act tough, though the truth was, I was scared shitless. But Lynette didn't seem fazed in the least: "You kiddin' me? I'm done with him. I'll tell him right to his face! Just let him try 'n' shoot me!"

She wasn't faking it. Lynette was a take-no-shit, eleven-going-on-eighteen, middle-school, Italian American version of Tina (Rosie Perez) in *Do the Right Thing*. But it wouldn't take long for me to see that she was as caring as she was fierce, just like the rest of the Solinas.

Lynette's parents grew up in the Pink Houses—a housing project in East New York, Brooklyn—but made their way to a co-op apartment in Hollis, Queens, just before Lynette and her two younger sisters were born. (Whether in East New York in the '70s or in Hollis in the '80s, the Solinas were one of the few Italian American families living in predominately African American neighborhoods.) John, Lynette's dad, managed the produce department at the King Kullen supermarket. Antonetta, her mom, worked part-time as a receptionist in a doctor's office on Hillside Avenue and part-time selling real estate but still made time to cook three-course Italian dinners most nights and full-on feasts on the weekends—beautifully arranged platters of antipasto, tray after tray of eggplant parmigiana, fresh pesto pasta, perfectly crisp breaded chicken cutlets, and homemade zeppoles for dessert.

The Solinas' dinner table on a Saturday night was the microcosm to the macrocosm of Queens—the most ethnically diverse, and delicious, place in the world. In addition to their family of five, Antonetta always extended an open invitation to their neighbors, their Brooklyn family, a bunch of Lynette's sisters' friends, and—by the end of sixth grade—Esther and me. The dinner table was right inside the front door to their apartment, which they kept unlocked for a good four hours on Saturday night, and every few minutes a new face poked in and everyone screamed, "HEY!," and then we all got up and jockeyed around the chairs until we were all eating elbow-to-elbow.

Even my mom got in on the action one night. And, soon afterward, she and Lynette's mom became as close friends as their daughters were. Antonetta and Carmella—seven syllables of pure Brooklyn Italian joy. And with that, the Solinas became, and remained, a second family to me.

By the start of seventh grade, Lynette, Esther, and I had anointed ourselves the L.E.T. crew—gel-curling our hair and tweezing our eyebrows together in our rooms after school, listening to Wreckx-N-Effect's "Rump Shaker" and Tupac's "I Get Around" on repeat. We weren't then, nor would we ever be, bad enough to actually graffiti our tag on brick walls, but we did take a can of black spray paint to a hidden back corner of my closet one day, spraying *L.E.T. Crew, L.E.T. Forever!* and *L.E.T.* inside a lightning bolt.

Throughout our years at MS 172 we were always more chess club than chain-link chokers—but we did catch one beef, with another group of girls, at the end of seventh grade. It never came to actual blows, if for no other reason than because Lynette was so willing to throw down. "What? You want to fight? So do it! Either you stop talking shit and just hit me, or we dead it! Enough with this in-between shit!"

Lynette fought fire with fire. Esther fought it by avoiding eye contact in the cafeteria. I fought it in a cloak of bad-girl style—I got the nameplate necklace, a name ring the next year, and continued to drive Dad bat-shit with my sneaker obsession. If all else failed, though, both Esther and I fought fire by standing back at a safe distance—which just meant, throughout the eighth grade and for pretty much the rest of our lives, anywhere behind Lynette.

13

The summer before I started high school, when I was four-teen, my mother planned a trip that—unbeknownst to me but not to her—was less a vacation than a pilgrimage. As with similar missions, Mom expected ours would bring about an awakening in me, although not one of the more typical spiritual or religious variety but, rather, the sexual type. Ergo, our destination wasn't Nazareth or Bethlehem or the remote burial site of some obscure Christian mar-tyr, but the grand sepulchre of all sexual inhibitions, the mausoleum of many a Midwestern boy's feigned interest in the NFL, that enormous tomb of all formerly closeted selves: the Great Gay Motherland of West Hollywood, Los Angeles. Mom was taking me to visit a living relic, otherwise known as her only lesbian friend, to see if basking in this friend's lavender light might make me realize what Mom had long since guessed was true: that I was one, too.

I had heard this friend's name mentioned over the years, but it wasn't until we were on the plane that she told me anything more substantial. It was Mom's freshman year at St. Joseph's College back in Brooklyn when she first met her—a sharp, rebellious, alcoholic, soon-to-be-heroin-addict, giant butch built of tough Rockaway Irish stock named, of all things, Rosemary. (That is not exactly how Mom described her, but that is exactly what she was. I know because, well, it takes one to know one, but—more blatantly—that's how she described herself. In fact, soon after we met, Rosemary told me that even being seen with an out butch lesbian in a Catholic school in 1960s Brooklyn was something none of the other girls was willing to do—Mom was her first, and only, college friend.)

As it turns out, my dad had met Rosemary in the Rockaway bar scene years before either of them met my mom, and Rosemary was the matchmaker on that fateful night at McNulty's. (Back then, as was the case years later, when Dad started hanging out with those few gay guy couples at Gregory's, the only qualification you needed for his friendship was the ability to handle your drinks and his jokes.)

By 1994, the year we flew across the country for a visit, Mom and Rosemary had been friends for over two decades. At some point in the last half of those twenty-plus years, Rosemary had sobered up and moved to L.A. . . . though I doubt in that order. She now had a job at "a shop." That seemingly inconsequential, but truly pivotal, tidbit was the last thing Mom said to me as we were de-boarding the plane. She mentioned it in passing, as in, "Dolly, Rosemary has to work today—and she works at a shop—so after we land, we'll go straight there and hang out till she gets off work. Okay?" I barely recall this detail registering with me, until, that is, our airport taxi pulled up in front of said "shop." After that point, I would never, ever forget it.

As Mom fiddled around in her purse to pay the cab driver, I just kept reading and rereading the shop sign, flashing back to Mom referencing "a shop," then rereading it again. I didn't entirely grasp what the words meant, but even so, I was pretty damn sure that whatever happened in the next ten minutes would be more interesting than anything that had happened in my fourteen years leading up to it. I blinked one more time to make sure I had it right. Yup, the sign read: 665: ONE STOP FROM HELL.

I recall the next five seconds like an out-of-body-experience, as if I were hovering over myself on Sunset

Boulevard looking down on it all: there I am, looking every bit the 1990s Queens teenage baby butch in my baggy jeans, all-black Raiders Starter jacket, and fresh Nike Air Trainer Huarache high-tops, feet frozen to the sidewalk, eyes like saucers. Then there's Mom, in her fanny pack and travel sweat suit, breaking into a run and jumping into the arms of this huge woman with a tattoo of a hypodermic needle and a metal spoon on her forearm with an X over it. "Rosemary!" Mom confirms.

As they twirl around and around in their bear hug, I finally work up the guts to take a few steps forward and sneak a peek into the shop window—turns out, *665: One Stop from Hell* is not a Californian pseudonym for the Department of Motor Vehicles. It is a sex-toy store, specifically the kind of sex-toy store that boasts a full rack of black leather harnesses and a hat stand draped with horse whips. (Despite the advanced education I was getting walking around Manhattan's West Village with my friends some Saturdays, it would be another decade before I'd learn that the term *S&M* could be used here.)

Rosemary gives me a quick shoulder pat and an "Eh, kid," then takes my luggage, wheels it into the store, parks it underneath a shelf stocked with foot-long black dildos, and turns to ask me if I'm hungry.

Though I can no longer speak, I manage to shake my head, *No.*

Mom, on the other hand, with a big ol' smile, says, "I could eat!"

I see them talking to each other, and then to me, but my brain is too overloaded to make meaning of the sounds; it's as if every last ounce of my cognitive functioning has been dedicated to deciphering the purpose of the many hundred silicone items of every conceivable shape and size looming over me from all directions. So instead of comprehensible language I hear, *"Meepy, meep're meep meep meep* across the *meep meep meep* sandwiches. *Meep meep* right *meep, meep* sit *meep!"* And before I understand what is happening, Mom and Rosemary walk out the shop door. Only after they're gone and I'm alone in the pristine silence of the sex-toy store am I able to process Mom's words: "Dolly, we're going to run across the street to get sandwiches. We'll be right back. Just sit there."

I slowly turn to the spot my mother was pointing to ten seconds ago—a high stool behind a glass case, on top of which is the cash register and displayed inside of which are neat rows of things that many years from now I will google to discover are called nipple clamps, ball stretchers, and pinwheels.

I open the case, pull out a pinwheel (it's like a pizza cutter but with pins instead of a blade) and run it up and down my arm. And then, I hear a familiar sound. *Ding-a-ling!* I look up toward the shop door with two simultaneous thoughts: 1) *You really don't expect one of those classic, cutesy doorbells in a shop like this—a little Bridgehampton candle store, sure, but here?* and 2) *That is definitely NOT Mom and Rosemary.*

Standing in front of me now is a couple in business suits, and they are very serious and focused, which may be why they don't realize that the person they're asking, "Where can we find the puppy cages?" is fourteen years old and has zero idea why they are asking that question here.

We stare at one another for the longest three seconds of my life. I imagine they're thinking something along the lines of: *I know that butch lesbians tend to look younger, what with their little-boy fashion sense, but this one takes the cake.* Meanwhile, I'm thinking: *Maybe they don't have Petco in California?*

Finally, they give up on the mute at the register and decide to go look for the cages on their own—665 isn't exactly Macy's, so they find them without much trouble. The moment they do, the woman drops down onto all fours and crawls inside one, while the guy, still standing, says, "Whattaya think of that, bitch?" She woofs; he says, "We'll take it."

As they walk out the door, he adds, "I can't exactly bring it back to the office, ha-ha, so we'll come by after work, and I'll pay for it then." And thank God for that, because I also don't know where to find the gift wrap.

Naturally, I head over to see this "puppy cage" but on my way get quickly distracted by what appears to be life-size G.I. Joe gear—*wait, are those gas masks?* One entire wall of the shop is dotted with hanging gas masks. And right away I feel the need to try one on, to see exactly what I would look like as a Cobra Viper.

I take down a mask, pull it over my head, tighten the straps, and walk over to the mirror to get a look at myself. After two, maybe three, steps, I realize I can't breathe. I try to get it off, but it won't budge. I'm pulling and pulling, fidgeting with the straps, twisting the cartridge in front, and nothing. I try to wedge my finger under the seal adhered to my face. Nothing. Now I'm in a full-on panic. I start whipping around the shop, arms flailing, trying to gasp, searching for something I could use to pry or smash it off with, but really I'm just going in circles until I'm in a total tailspin, looking like a postapocalyptic version of the Tasmanian devil trapped in a sex-toy store.

I make it to the mirror and start banging my head into it, hoping that will break the gas mask open—no such luck. Then, with what feels like my very last breath eking out of my nose, at long last, I hear it ... *ding-a-ling!*—and my mother and Rosemary burst through the shop door.

They charge toward me, throwing their sandwiches into the air. Everything starts to go into slow motion, as I spend what I imagine are my few remaining seconds of consciousness in this world, struck not by the fear of encroaching death, but by the insanity of the fact that the very last thing I might ever see would be from behind the lens of a gas mask that's suffocating me in front of my mother and her butchy best friend in the sex-toy shop the latter manages for a living, which I was left alone to run, at fourteen, all within the first hour of my first visit to L.A.

I don't mean to spoil the surprise, but I survived. In fact, I didn't even lose consciousness—with a lightning-fast, two-handed twist-and-pull combo move, Rosemary shelled that gas mask from my head as if my skull were a peanut. Somehow, in a remarkably short amount of time, Mom, Rosemary, and I just moved on, chitchatting away as if 665 was our favorite café, as if nothing had ever happened, as if this hadn't been the single strangest sixty minutes of my entire life. But while I leapt seamlessly from meeting the puppy cage couple to the typical teenage talk of school and friends, I was later to learn that Mom and Rosemary were sweating buckets, shocked that they had dodged this particular bullet and managed to steer things back on track.

It would be years before she told me, but it turned out that my mother had ZERO idea that Rosemary worked in an S&M shop until the very second the cab that had brought us there pulled away from outside 665. She had written down the address but not the name of the store and was so focused on paying the taxi driver that she had yet to read the sign until the cab took off. Rosemary had sworn up and down that she'd told Mom the kind of shop she worked in and didn't question it much when Mom said we would come there from the airport, because she had it in her head that I was a lot older than I was.

Regardless, the second I walked off to peer into the shop window, Mom and Rosemary, still hugging, were sharing panicked whispers, trying to figure out what the hell to do. Mom had a split second to make a tough decision: her whole plan was to introduce me to a lesbian friend, to show me that she had one, and thereby impress upon me that it was perfectly okay for me to be one, and she couldn't figure out how to say, "Actually, we're not going into my friend's workplace, even though we are standing right in front of it," without also really confusing me and making the whole start of our trip supremely uncomfortable. More than anything, she deduced, it wasn't worth foiling her entire plan just to avoid fielding a few questions about sex toys. So she decided to go in the complete opposite direction and pretend this was the most normal establishment in the world. She leapt at the chance to grab those sandwiches to powwow with Rosemary on her decision, never imagining that both the puppy cage and gas mask incidents would happen within the mere ten minutes they were gone.

After Rosemary's shift was over, she took us to a kitschy family restaurant called The Stinking Rose, where every item on the menu was garlic-based, even the ice cream. We three sat there sharing a bowl, taking turns lifting the tiniest possible spoonfuls into our mouths and wincing, looking not unlike any of the other adorable families around us (but with one hell of a better backstory).

We drove to Rosemary's apartment in her low-rider Caddy with chrome rims—apparently she had really taken to L.A. culture—and she went extra fast and rolled down all the windows and I asked if I could wear her leather jacket, claiming "I'm getting kinda cold ..." But I wasn't.

She gave me a wink and draped it over my shoulders, and I stuck my face out the car window into the wind, feeling in awe of Rosemary, her jacket, her car, and her wallet chain. In other words, I felt the very draw to this person that my mother had presumed I would ... even if it would be another five years before I had any clue as to why.

14

Six months after I left L.A., by some sick miracle I once again found myself in a self-induced near-death situation that involved both a thugged-out best friend and gas masks—well, more like an event at which everyone was praying they had one of the latter. It also just so happened to take place in another place popular among sadists: Catholic school.

Several things had to happen for me to end up there. My zoned public high school had such a bad reputation (with newly installed metal detectors to confirm that said reputation was well deserved) that, come eighth grade, all my friends at Middle School 172 were desperate to find an alternative. A few lucky kids passed the test to get into one of the city's super-competitive specialized public high schools (e.g., Stuyvesant, Brooklyn Tech, Bronx Science). Esther and Lynette were headed to Bayside High, a public school a few neighborhoods over that admitted out-of-district students to their arts program, and I might well have convinced my parents to let me join them had I not cut school the day of the aforementioned entry tests. In so doing, I not only lost my chance to attend one of those top schools, but I also managed to convince my parents that what I needed more than the company of my best friends, a rigorous academic program, or an arts education was the drilling of hard-nosed nuns.

In 1994, the going tuition rate for a New York City Catholic high school was around $4,000 a year—a price that most cop/construction worker/car mechanic dads in my chunk of Queens could afford, and one-tenth the cost of other private schools. For the money, Catholic schools offered a slightly better education than your average public school, though not half as good as the specialized ones. But whatever these institutions may have lacked in academics, they made up for by way of discipline—and by greatly reducing your kid's chances of being shot. And so, much to my dismay, I was headed for St. Mary's.

To make matters worse, the only other MS 172 kid set to do a stint at St. Mary's was one I didn't like. Alli was the epitome of the popular, pretty, mean girl, which in Queens of 1994 meant she was something like the love child of Barbie and Snoop Dogg. A thugged-out Irish girl with gel-curled long blond hair, brown lipstick, a perpetual scowl, and too-tight clothes, she had grown up down the block from me on 253rd Street, attended all the same schools I had from kindergarten on up, and had her Holy Communion and Confirmation at St. Greg's, like I did. And yet, at fourteen years old, having been in the same place practically every day for nine straight years, we had never spoken a word to each other.

After the L.A. trip, I started to veer from the standard Queens kid hip-hop look to some combo of the grunge fashion I saw on MTV (and not anywhere else around me) and the "Rosemary/Still Unaware Little Lesbian Chic." I kept rocking fresh sneakers, but as the other girls' jeans got tighter and tighter, I started to wear mine baggy, pairing them with thermal or flannel shirts. And though I could still recite every Wu-Tang Clan lyric, I started seeking out classic punk and rock music—nearly all my peers listened exclusively to rap and hip-hop, and it would be many more years before I had any idea that in the larger world they were not the rule but the exception and that outside Queens I wouldn't have been the only teenager in a ten-mile radius who owned a Jimi Hendrix album.

Alli dismissed people like me as too weird and uncool

to even bother with; I dismissed her as unoriginal and unintelligent. But, despite our protests, our dads—who were both cops and had long been pretty friendly—forced a get-together on us. A few weeks before school started, for the first time ever, I was to walk the three hundred feet from my house on 253rd down to hers, so "you two can spend a little time, get to know each other ... won't kill yuhs!" Dad said.

I thought it would be just us, but when I got there, she was waiting out front with a little crew of girl clones—all wearing painted-on, cutoff jean short-shorts, baby tees, door-knockers, and all-white low-top Reebok Classics. Beside them was a pair of guys with matching Caesar haircuts and plaid boxers sticking out from jeans belted below their asses. Nobody said a word when they saw me but instantly took off in a pack, all behind Alli. She turned back and said, "You comin' or not?" I rolled my eyes, feeling as if I had just walked into some lame-ass after-school special, but followed them anyway, all the way to the back corner of the handball court at the PS 133 playground.

I had never smoked weed before, but I sure as shit didn't say that, and when the blunt came my way, I took a long, proper puff, hunching over and pulling from my toes so I wouldn't cough and face hell before passing it to Alli. After she took her hit, she looked me up and down, and said, "Why are you so fucking weird? I mean, 'grunge,' or whatever might be cool in Bubbafuck, Kansas, or some shit . . . but here it's just wack." To which I shot back, "Says the girl whose ass cheeks are hanging out of her shorts like some—" I stopped myself as Alli, now all cocked head and pursed lips, squared up to me as if she was going to throw a punch if I let slip a single syllable more.

I took a step back but, suddenly struck with the feeling that this was one of those fork-in-the-road, fight-or-flight, pivotal life moments, dug deep to summon my inner Lynette Solina and stepped forward again, chin up. I changed course but didn't back down. "Besides, that doesn't make any sense. I think you mean, Bubbafuck, *Seattle*."

"Seattle, Kansas—what's the fucking difference?"

"Damn, you really gotta get out of New York. Or buy a map."

"They got a *Bubbafuck* atlas?"

"Yeah. You never heard of it? The Big Book of *Bubbafucks*."

And at the same time that the tension broke, the weed kicked in, and we both started laughing so hard, we keeled over. Then we hooked arms to use each other as leverage to get to our feet, and that was that.

For the next few years we began every single day this

way: arms hooked, crying-laughing over one stupid thing or another, smoking a blunt for breakfast, walking down our block to get the bus to school. By our sophomore year, however, we weren't getting on the bus to St. Mary's anymore—after we instigated that near-death situation, we got kicked out.

A month into my freshman year, I had proven to be the type of high school student who—if I wasn't asleep or stoned during class—I was drunk. In the waistband of my uniform's pleated wool skirt, I kept a "flask" of whiskey, which I'd made by washing out a travel-size shampoo bottle a thousand times (and then I colored it with a gold paint marker). Whenever I drank from it, I thought I was Janis Joplin reincarnate.

Meanwhile, in the waistband of Alli's skirt, rolled up to shorten its length to all of four inches and always worn with thigh-highs, was a beeper that went off incessantly with the stream of guys she was flirting with but never talked about.

By this time, Alli and I were inseparable. I loved her brand of toughness, and she loved mine. I loved how smart she was, even if she didn't want anyone to know it. I loved that, as hard as Alli worked to keep everyone else at arm's distance, she pulled me in close, twice as hard. And yet, for all the time we spent together, all the bus rides, lunch-times, weeknights, and weekend conversations, sex was the one thing we didn't speak about—in fact, even though it wasn't difficult to guess that she had some experience, I only learned the extent of it by accident.

Half-drunk at 3:00 p.m. and lollygagging along at Al-li's side as we walked toward the bus stop after school one day, out of nowhere I heard, "You little bitch! I know what you did! Stop!" We both turned back to see a gang of senior girls a block away but gaining on us, the two at the front shouting to their crew, "That's the fucking freshman who screwed my boyfriend!" "Yeah, mine, too! I'm gonna kill her!"

Just then the bus appeared at the corner, and Alli put her hand on my back, pushed me forward, and took off running toward it, "We gotta book! There's too many of 'em! GO!"

Alli gave them double fuck-you fingers through the bus window as we pulled away, then took a seat and made as if nothing had happened. I was confused as all hell, but right then I remembered walking into her house the previous Saturday night, just as two guys I kind of recognized were walking out. As soon as I saw her that night, in her room, I said, "Who were they?"

"Nobody," she said. And I'd left it alone. But this time I couldn't.

"Those boys, from last week—they were seniors?"

"Uh-huh."

"You never said you . . . I mean, how'd you meet them anyway?"

"School."

"Yeah, I got that part . . . So did you? I mean, you hooked up with both of—"

"That's none of your fucking business."

"Okay. Fine. But—"

"But what!? You wanna sit around talking about first-, second-base bullshit, all huddled up in the cafeteria, giggling, like some teen girls on TV shit?"

"No. But I also don't want to get my ass kicked, so maybe you should tell—"

"I'll handle it tomorrow—trust me."

"Okay. I guess, I also just want to know if . . . you're okay?"

"I'm fine. Leave it."

I have no idea when or how, but Alli managed to do something to make those girls leave us alone forever after. And, as she clearly wanted, I never brought any of it up again. Even so, for me, there would always be this unresolved internal debate: on the one hand, I loved that Alli alone seemed to burst the stereotype of teen girls sharing every detail of their budding sex lives with one another, of needing to get approval on whether they should or shouldn't do this or that, or of talking about sex incessantly because they thought it made them look cool. She just went out and did whatever she did with whomever she pleased, and she neither bragged about it, nor was ashamed. At times, I told myself, *She's just more mature than everyone else. She's a badass. She can handle it.* At other times, the fact that it seemed to me that she had more sexual experience at fourteen than most people do at thirty straight-out worried me sick. In retrospect, I should have said as much, but when it came down to it, some part of me lacked the nerve to question her. Besides, initiating any further conversation about sex put me in danger of having my own feelings on the subject examined, and, though I really didn't know what they were just yet, I knew I didn't want them analyzed.

Halfway into our freshman year, Alli and I were spending so much time together that her little crew of girl clones from the neighborhood hardly ever came around anymore. Thanks to something of a perfect storm—being in different schools, my wanting to be with Alli all weekend, and their disapproval of all the drinking and weed-smoking I was doing—for a bit I saw a lot less of Esther and Lynette.

Alli had let her guard down around me in a way I hadn't seen her do before or since; but even when you lifted the chain mail, she was still a pit bull underneath it. Yet every once in a while, if we were alone in my room, she'd lie belly up on the carpet, high and silly, eating Cheez Doodles, telling me my Rancid album "isn't that wack, I guess, but Biggie is up next," and for at least a few minutes, she looked like the fourteen-year-old girl you could sometimes forget she was.

While other teenage best friends expressed their mutual love by writing their names in their notebooks with *BFF* underneath, Alli's way of showing me she cared was by threatening to beat up a girl who ratted on me for smoking in the bathroom. She didn't tell me she was going to do it. I came out of class to find Alli waiting, dead silent, arms crossed, eyeing the girl down. Then, without a word to me, she stepped up to her and said, "If you ever mess with my friend again, I will fuck you up." The girl burst into tears, and Alli hooked her arm under mine, and we walked away. It was the closest thing I ever got to an "I love you."

For six straight months we hardly spent more than a few hours apart, and yet Alli and I still looked like the types of girls who not only sit at different tables in the cafeteria, but who spend the entire lunch period sneering at each other, mutually enraged by the other's mere existence. But there we were, day in, day out, at our very own table, alone, together.

Our sole common bond was the love of trouble, as well as a shared disdain for sobriety, and we egged each other on to start as much of the first and have as little of the second as possible, though we weren't competing against each other as much as we were a tag team versus badasses the world over.

She kept us constantly supplied with weed and cigarettes, while I plotted each new scheme, hiking up the risk factor every go-round: "It's 1:00 a.m., and my mom is sound asleep; let's take her car for a spin around the block! Now let's take it on the highway and see how fast we can go. Now that the Pizza Hut lot is frozen over with ice thanks to this blizzard, let's drive over there and do donuts. Now let's drive all the way into Manhattan and back. Now let's drive all the way to Manhattan, park in a garage, laugh our asses off when the attendant points to the Yellow Pages in the driver's seat (I couldn't see out the windshield without it) and asks, 'You sure you're old enough to drive?' then go to a club with our fake IDs, drive home high and drunk just after 4:00 a.m., park the car exactly as we found it, and tiptoe back to bed so that our parents will be none the wiser." (And they weren't.)

Having gotten away with so much legitimately illegal activity for so long, it came as a shock to both of us that what started out as one of our lesser, impromptu, in-school pranks our freshman year was what finally got us in some real trouble.

We were sitting together in the science lab when I launched the plan:

"*Psst.* Yo, Al?"

"Yo."

"You see that, the pipe, in the back?"

"The red one, with the steering wheel thing at the top?"

"Uh-huh. I'm guessing that's the gas line for the spigot things on our desks. Think I'm right?"

"Probably. So what?"

"I'm gonna turn it on, get us all out of class!"

"How the hell you gettin' up there without Sammut seeing you?"

"You jump up on the desk, start dancing around like crazy to distract him, and then I'll shimmy up the pipe. Cool?"

"A'ight. Fuck it."

For the first five minutes afterward everything went according to plan: she danced, I shimmied, the gas came out of the spigots, Mr. Sammut screamed bloody blue murder at Alli and me, then chucked our backpacks out the classroom door and into the hall and told us to pick them up on our way to the principal's office. As soon as we cleared the doorway, we cracked up, but ten seconds later an announcement came over the loudspeakers: "Teachers and staff, please usher all students out of the building to the yard immediately. This is not a drill," followed by the full blast of the school fire alarms. We stopped dead, let out an "Oh, shit" in tandem, then turned on our heels and ran straight out the front door of the school to the street. We kept going until we ran out of breath.

It wasn't until later that night, when Brother George (the principal) called our parents, that we got the full story: the sophomore chemistry class was in the adjoining lab using the Bunsen burners at the very same time that our classroom was filling with gas. When the teacher in that class heard Mr. Sammut's screams, then saw some of the burners in her lab flickering strangely, she knew something was up and thought fast. She shut off the gas in her room, opened the windows, and called the school office. Thanks to that there wasn't a huge explosion, but we still became known as "the girls who blew up the lab," and our parents were told to find us another school.

15

It's closing in on 8:00 a.m., and it's mayhem inside the no-name bodega on 179th Street and Hillside Avenue. Like peasants in revolt, the mob at the front counter pump their plastic packages of Drake's Cakes, Little Debbie Honey Buns, and wax-paper-wrapped buttered rolls in the air, waiting for the guy behind the register to point at them and scream, "Fifty cents! . . . Seventy-five! . . . Buck fifty!" before they slap down their stacks of coins and bulldoze out the door. In the back, it's three-deep at the deli counter, heads popping up and down like the moles in Whac-A-Mole: Up on tiptoe to place an order—"Lemme getta bacon, egg, and cheese, salt/pepper/hot sauce!" "Coffee, light and sweet!" "Make that two!"; going back down to wait; up again when the guy calls out that it's ready, to yells of "Yo! That's mine!"; back down as a chain of out-stretched hands crowd-surfs the food to the waiting customer. And though the breakfasts may differ, every single one of those hands belongs to a teenage girl, each one unique with regard to the severity of her *Don't fuck with me* stare, or her lack or overabundance of gold jewelry and makeup, or whether she has a penchant for airbrushed fingernails, but all of them wearing identical white button-down shirts, pleated wool skirts, and matching vests.

When the girls empty back out to the street, they're joined by hundreds more climbing up from the F train station or out of any one of dozens of city buses, together forming an impenetrable conveyor belt of Queens Catholic school girls streaming down Hillside, past the check-cashing place, the OTB, the 99-cent store, and the hole-in-the-wall Caribbean and Chinese restaurants, before turning the corner onto 178th, a quiet side street that climbs a supersteep hill, at the top of which, in a beige brick Gothic building surrounded by spiky black cast-iron fencing, loomed the Mary Louis Academy, my and Alli's second high school. On a really, really good day it looked like Camelot . . . and on all the other ones, Alcatraz.

In lieu of King Arthur or wardens, Mary Louis was home to the Sisters of St. Joseph order of nuns, and in lieu of Lancelot or inmates, the Academy boasted a volatile mix of Queens girls from all corners of the borough— bad girls from good neighborhoods, good girls from bad ones, and the ultra-religious from both. We were the New Yorkers who never make it into the popular imaginings of our city: hard-ass Filipinos with thick Queens accents, loud-mouthed Koreans drinking Tropical Fantasy soda, Colombian goths, prudish Puerto Ricans hunched under enormous backpacks, their white uniform shirts buttoned all the way to the neck. Miraculously, most of us got along, and all of us were the better for being sequestered.

There were several factions of Irish/Italian girls at Mary Louis, and within the first few weeks at our new school, in September 1995, Alli and I found our rightful place with the toughest ones. There was Lisa, an Italian, who beat out even Alli in the contests for the shortest skirt, longest fake nails, and brownest lipstick—the way she carried herself, if it weren't for the uniform, you'd have sworn she was thirty. And Erin and Claire, two first-generation Irish girls who spent their Saturdays at a local pub in Woodside, where, come ten o'clock, all the hard-drinking old men in tweed caps were replaced by dozens of young teenagers lined up on stools with their money on the bar, ordering rounds like pros. And then there was Kristy, who lived alone with her dad, a sweet-hearted construction worker she loved dearly but who was an on-again, off-again drug addict.

At fifteen, Alli and I were still finding trouble *after* school—smoking blunts in the park with her new boyfriend and his crew, sneaking out to clubs in the city with our new school friends—but we weren't doing half-bad during the day. We showed up on time; we did just enough to pass our classes; we didn't blow anything up.

I was still a frenetic, mischievous ball of energy, hyped up on my daily breakfast of weed and Tropical Fruit Starburst, but, thanks to a collaborative intervention by Alli and Mom, I had since ditched the travel-shampoo flask. After a year of my drinking from it all day and then really going overboard at parties come Saturday night, one day Alli gave me an ultimatum: "For real, you're crazy with the drinking! Either you quit, or I'm telling your mother." (It should be noted that Alli wouldn't have dreamed of ratting on anyone with any other mom, but she truly loved and trusted mine, and she knew I did, too—it's not all that common for little hooligans to also be mama's girls, but I was one. Shit, I still am.)

Turned out, I didn't have to make that choice. One night I came home so wasted, Mom found me throwing up in the bathroom. When it was over, she didn't yell, she just patted my forehead with a towel and said, "Oh, my Chickenella, how long has this been going on?" I told her. She cupped my face with her hands and said, "It's time to stop." And I did—by the time I turned sixteen, that May, I hadn't had a drink for a year.

I was still smoking my weight in weed and cigarettes, though, and right before the end of sophomore year, when I headed into the bathroom in between classes for my usual smoke, I found Kristy, locked in a stall, bawling. She didn't say anything at first but waved me over, opened her school bag, and pointed to a resin-stained glass pipe.

"I found it in his room. It's a crack pipe, right?"

"Oh, shit. I mean, yeah, I think so. Whattaya gonna do?"

"Dunno … but you gotta promise me you won't say anything, okay?"

"Okay. For sure, I promise." Bell.

Kristy never cut classes, but she didn't move.

"Yo, you comin'?"

She shook her head. No.

Right before I walked out the bathroom door, I looked back, hoping she had changed her mind. That image of her, with her back to me, staring out the bathroom window, clutching her school bag to her chest, wrecks my head something fierce, even today.

Immediately afterward, Kristy took on a full-time night job as a gym receptionist to pay the rent, since she knew her dad wouldn't be able to cover it. The job left her so tired during the day that she'd sleep straight through lunch, head down on our cafeteria table. Still, for fear of getting him in trouble if the school administration or his construction boss caught wind of his using, she didn't tell anyone she was working nights, not even us, for over a year.

Kristy's secret was mighty big, but she certainly wasn't the only girl in our group to have one—who was dating a twenty-five-year-old, whose dad had mob ties, whose brother was locked up . . . these secrets mostly stayed hidden for many years. But then, one came along that couldn't be kept for more than a few months. In the summer between our sophomore and junior year, just after her sixteenth birthday, Alli found out she was pregnant.

Squatting in front of a bookshelf with a stolen cup of coffee, I tilted my head like a dog at a shadow. Ear to shoulder, eyebrows raised, I mouthed the title of a book I'd never seen before: *K-I-N-G L-E-A-R*.

Huh. Must be some Knights of the Round Table type-a-thing, I figured.

Straightaway I pulled the book from the shelf and split it open, not looking to read it so much as to perform an autopsy. I had smuggled the coffee from the teachers' lounge and had to stay hidden in a rarely used classroom to drink it. I was hoping for pictures or some chivalric bit of nonsense to help me pass the time. Instead, there on the page was line after line of language as beautiful as it was bizarre, and I was mesmerized. I plopped down, crossed my legs on the cold linoleum, and turned to the beginning. Act One. Scene One.

I was at the tail end of my junior year, and I had never read a book on my own. But I kept at this one in a fury, cutting one class after the next after the next, until I was done.

After the end-of-school bell, I put the book back on the shelf, peeled my legs off the floor, and rushed to catch the bus, excited to find my friends at the bus stop on Hillside and tell them about what I had read.

From my preferred center seat in the last row of the Q43, I started to recount the story. For this particular stretch, Hillside was more than just a major avenue; it was also the dividing line between one of the poorest neighborhoods in the borough, Jamaica, and one of the richest, Jamaica

Estates. Outside the right window scrolled tree-lined streets filled with English Tudor–style mansions, and outside the left, garbage swirled up the stoops of dilapidated clapboard houses, while I talked about "this crazy old motherfucker" and his "two grubby, bitch-ass daughters."

When madmen lead the blind . . .

No one gave a crap.

Just a few months earlier, on March 4, 1996, I had been in that very same seat on the Q43, but I was heading in the opposite direction, in every sense—instead of synopsizing Shakespeare for my uninterested friends, I was alone, cutting school to go to Jamaica Hospital and meet Alli's newborn daughter.

Sister Joan, our principal, along with Alli's parents, decided that Alli would stay in school until she started "showing," which worked out to right until Christmas break. After that, she'd do her schoolwork from home. I still saw her almost every day, after school, but instead of talking about the next party or prank, we were talking about baby clothes, baby strollers, diapers, and Alli's boyfriend, the baby's father. He had dropped out of high school, claiming he had gotten a job to take care of Alli and their daughter. But she had her doubts.

As soon as I walked into her hospital room, Alli said, "Go call his ass now!"

I called from the waiting room, then from home the next day, and the next, and the next. He never called back.

As flies to wanton boys.

With so much of Alli's future suddenly so indelibly written, it soon occurred to me that I should start working out my own. Up until she got pregnant, neither she nor I thought much beyond the next blunt in the park. My mother wanted me to go to college, but my father often said he would have been fine with me going into the police academy or even the army. I wasn't sure about any of it, until I read *King Lear.*

I ran home from the bus that day and straight to my room, grabbing my mother's stack of old magazines and a pair of scissors on the way, and set out to make a collage based on the themes of the book. I had done very few of my assignments for English class and hoped this would count for something to my teacher. In the middle of a sheet of paper I glued a King of Hearts playing card and surrounded it with phrases like *twisted sister.* For the first time, I cared about something that could be called schoolwork.

The next day I stood at my teacher's desk, too giddy to keep up my typical tough-girl act, and started to explain to her, "So I read this book yesterday—I don't know if you've heard of it—*King Lear*? And, uh—"

"Cut the crap, Clancy. No, you didn't."

"What? Um, yes, I did." She rolled her eyes, but I was undeterred. "Anyway, so I made this . . ."

"Shakespeare. Yesterday, after not doing any work all year, you up and read Shakespeare, for the hell of it? And, wait, the whole play, no less? C'mon, kid! I'm not an idiot."

At that I slapped my collage onto her desk and walked off. The next day she slapped it back onto my desk, upside-down so I could read her note right away: *A++ This is fantastic!* Then she said, "Let's talk after class today, okay?" I gave a smug smile, followed by a real one, and nodded.

The following summer, before senior year, instead of playing handball at the PS 133 park with me, Alli was pushing a stroller around it. Sometimes I'd join her for a loop or two, and we'd catch up; other times, she'd come over to my house and we'd fight over music and eat Cheez Doodles as always, only now we were also taking turns cradling the baby.

Come the start of the school year, Alli's mom had

agreed to babysit during the day—she did administrative work at our local police precinct and was able to switch her schedule, buying Alli just enough time to rush straight home after school and pick up her daughter before her mom had to leave for her shift. And on nights and weekends, Alli got a job waiting tables—she was a seventeen-year-old single mom, and she was as dedicated a mother as one twice her age. One day, when it was just the three of us in my room, I couldn't help breaking our badass code to tell her how impressed I was, "I'm so fucking proud of you! You're like Mary Poppins but sluttier."

In jest, there is truth . . .

"Oh, shit. You wanna get smart?! Don't think I can't hold this baby with one hand and knock your ass out with the other!"

Who is it that can tell me who I am?

"Ha! There's my girl! But, for real, Al, you're one helluva mom."

"Thanks, girl. Now that's enough with the mushy shit!"

Speak what we feel, not what we ought to say.

Thanks to that *King Lear*–collage-induced chat with my junior-year English teacher, I started senior year in an

AP class devoted to Shakespeare—this Fool had finally found her place, and I never missed another assignment.

And, while even motherhood couldn't turn Alli from a Mae West to a Donna Reed, there was no doubting that she had changed some. One day, just a few weeks into the school year, sitting next to me in the cafeteria, she leaned to whisper into my ear.

"*Psst.* Yo, I got an idea. Howsa about we do one last thing before we leave this hellhole, to give 'em something to remember us by!"

"Uh-oh. What?"

"Let's make the honor roll! Actually, nah, fuck that— the dean's list! C'mon!"

"You serious?"

"Dead ass."

". . . A'ight, fuck it."

So, we did.

Alli's parents were so thrilled by our semester of straight A's, they decided to babysit her daughter so she could go to prom. She was beside herself, even if she would have to come straight home afterward and not join the rest of our crew at the after-party. Somebody had found a cheap little house near the beach out east, and we calculated, if we pooled together all our summer and weekend job money, we had just enough for a two-night stay.

It had to be paid for, in full, two weeks in advance, and we made it just in time. And then, just a week before prom, we got the news: this cheap house was too cheap to be true. We had been scammed. All our money was gone.

I had been so solidly schooled by my mother to be proud of what we had, that what was ours was ours and what was his was his, that a few more days would pass before the thought even occurred to me. I went to Mom first, and with her okay, I decided to call Mark. I wasn't but a quarter of the way into the story when he cut me off—

"The house is all yours."

He really meant it, too. Mark decided to stay on Roosevelt Island so we could have the Bridgehampton place all to ourselves. And come prom weekend, there was Kristy, Erin, and the rest of our crew, one by one, doing cannonballs into the lagoon pool.

16

"If I told you that the universe was infinite," Mark says, "that it had NO END ..." He was now leaning so far back into his chair that the front two legs came off the floor, and all six feet, ten inches of him was teetering on the back two—the international symbol for *Get ready, this one's gonna take a while*—"... how would that make you feel?"

And, particularly in this scenario, he was not being overly dramatic—a question like that would take a while for anyone to answer. But it's especially the case for me, because I'm five years old.

As far back as I can remember, Mark had a strict dinner itinerary: Cocktail hour. Appetizers. Salad course. Entrée. Dessert. Existential Questions.

And, as far back as I can remember, I'd just as soon skip the soufflé and get right to the conversation.

If we were at Mark's Roosevelt Island apartment, we had these talks in his Victorian-era-inspired sitting area, sitting in tufted leather wingback chairs—for him, think Woody Allen's head on Larry Bird's body hosting Masterpiece Theatre; for me, think a dangling, squeaky-voiced, anthropomorphic pair of Nikes talking the cosmos (I was so engulfed by that giant chair, all you could see of me in profile were my shoes).

The chairs sat in front of Mark's enormous wraparound living room windows that, seventeen stories up, provided a panoramic view of the Manhattan skyline. Rapt in thought, I'd stare out at the zillion lights, while Mozart's Symphony No. 40 or Beethoven's Ninth lulled and swelled in the background. Or, if my little brain really went into overdrive and I needed a break, mid-conversation I'd reach for the windowsill to snatch up Mark's jumbo pair of vintage black binoculars—like two liters of Coca-Cola strapped to my little face—and zoom in on a guy in his Midtown kitchen, or a couple walking arm in arm along the Manhattan waterfront, or the cars crossing the Queensboro Bridge. *Whew, space may be expanding, but so long as that guy is picking his nose in his Chevy, I can be sure of my existence.*

If we were in Bridgehampton, we were always tucked into the pine wormwood table near the kitchen, under the upended antique radio horn turned hanging lamp, catty-corner from the brick fireplace and the room-long, grid-paned window, on the other side of which was that giant ancient elm tree and the country night sky—same zillion lights, same little brain in overdrive, but here, instead of Mozart, an equally potent concerto of crickets, crackling firewood, and Mark's teetering chair creaking away on the old farmhouse floorboards. (Mark didn't allow music in Bridgehampton, with the exception of weekends when his best friend, my Uncle Sal, and his crew were visiting, in which case he not only permitted but enjoyed our Riccobono family ritual of all-out Motown dance parties, where we'd stagger ourselves on the staircase, begin our slow, finger-snapping descent, then start belting out the Temptations' "Ain't Too Proud to Beg," using Mark's eighteenth-century brass candle snuffers as makeshift microphones.)

When it was just the three of us, Mark and I would go on and on talking for so long after dessert in Bridge-hampton that Mom would leave us to it and head to bed. But at some stage she'd crack her bedroom door and yell, "Bedtime, Chickenella!" Then I'd beg for more existential

conversation the same way I begged Dad to let me watch
one more episode of *He-Man* in Broad Channel or pleaded
with Grandma to let me play one more game of Ollie Ollie
Oxen Free: "Just five more minutes, Ma! Please!"

One of those times, when I was about ten, Mom gave in,
but when five minutes turned to thirty, she plodded down
the stairs, all groggy and squinty-eyed in her nightgown,
and, shocked to see us still going strong, said, "Are you
two gonna talk about the moon and stars ALL NIGHT?"

And that's how these marathon conversations got their
name—forever after we called them our "moon and stars
talks."

Prior to prom weekend, none of my friends at Mary Louis
had any real idea what it meant when I turned down in-
vitations to hang out because I was "going to my mom's
boyfriend's place." Alli had met Mark not long into our
friendship, a few years earlier, at my house on 253rd Street
in Queens, and I'm sure that I told her a rough version of
my backstory, but she wasn't the type to ask a lot of questions, and I didn't go into details. As for the rest of my

friends, if I glazed over the specifics, it wasn't because I was trying to hide any details so much as they weren't exactly easy to work into cafeteria conversation. "Hey, Tara. Everybody's goin' to the park Saturday, smoke a couple blunts, chill. You comin?"

What was I supposed to say?: *"Well, I was planning on discussing the Hudson River School painters, maybe a little particle physics, for hours and hours, like I've been doing since I was five, with my mom's boyfriend, Mark, who, I guess I haven't mentioned, is this rich genius giant, literally, and he has this insane duplex in the city—which my mom used to clean; that's how they met—as well as this extraordinary Bridgehampton estate, but he's otherwise just another member of our big Italian Brooklyn family! And we don't take any money from him, but he's supergenerous in so many other ways, and he would give it to us if we asked, but we don't, ever, because my mom really values her autonomy, and so even though they've been together for almost my whole life, they've never gotten married or lived together, and Mom and I have always stayed right here in Queens, and I'm pretty much just like all of you ..." bell rings ...* Ah, to hell with it.

"Blunts, Saturday, see you then!"

By fourteen, I actually was choosing weed in Queens over existential conversation in the Hamptons pretty regularly. Up until then I had been with Mark and Mom every other weekend, but now my mom would allow me to opt out and stay over at Alli's or another friend's house instead. Also, years earlier, come the end of Middle School 172, just as the full-blown, *Great Gatsby*–esque, airborne, Riccobono-invasion parties had stopped, so, too, did the limos arriving to pick me up from school—if one had pulled up in front of the bodega on 179th and Hillside, there was no way I could have gone three minutes, let alone three years, without an explanation.

At seventeen, I had only two friends who fully knew the details of my social-strata–hopping life: Esther and Lynette. When I told Esther, at eight, I was so young, I was not at all conscious that it could be perceived as strange. As she was the same age, she hardly batted an eye. "Oh, okay, cool. So, you wanna play Miss Mary Mack now?" Telling Lynette at age twelve was a different story.

There were two reasons it wasn't difficult explaining why my mom didn't take any money from Mark. One was that by the time I was in middle school, my mom had left her job waiting tables at The Old Tubby House after landing a much more lucrative sales position at AT&T—we

were by no means rolling in it, but we had as much, if not more, than most of my friends' families. And two, even if my friends didn't perceive us as comfortable, it was never hard to explain to anyone in Queens, young or old, then or now, my mom's insistence on being self-supporting.

That said, then, the problem when I first told Lynette about my quasi dual life wasn't the money . . . it was the ketchup.

By age twelve, I was very much aware that the way things worked at Mark's house was different from what my friends were used to, and, before the first time I brought Lynette to Bridgehampton for the weekend, I felt the need to prepare her. At that stage, the priority in those preparations was explaining that Mark didn't allow ketchup, or any other condiment, to be placed on the dinner table in its original packaging. So, the Friday before we were to leave, in the recess yard of MS 172, while the other kids were beating the snot out of one another on one side, on the other I huddled up with Lynette.

"Well, if I can't put the ketchup on the table, where the hell do I put it? The floor?"

"You have to take it out of the bottle and put it in a ramekin, with a little spoon."

"A ram-e-what?"

"It's like a bowl, a porcelain one, with ridges on it. Don't worry, I'll show you."

"Huh. So long as I get to go in that pool, I'll put the ketchup wherever he wants!"

Come the end of our eighth-grade summer, at age fourteen, Lynette had spent so much time in Bridgehampton that when Mark invited her whole family for a weekend, she took great pride in giving them a tour of the property herself. "And this is the Barn . . . and Mark calls this the Main House . . . and here's the kitchen, and—wait, see these things? These are what we use for ketchup, mustard, everything—they're called ramekins."

Not long after that weekend, Mark started offering the Solinas his house for a whole week every year. He insisted on staying on Roosevelt Island so that they could have the run of the place, and though he and Mom weren't there, I was. I can't remember whether, without Mark around, they put the ketchup bottle on the table, but I do have a favorite memory of watching John Solina, Lynette's dad and a second father to me, with a deep tan and a wide smile, wearing his classic Italian man's slip-on white leather Keds and a tank top, walking back up Jobs Lane from the beach midmorning, just past Colin Powell's house, fishing rod in one hand, tackle box swinging from the other, bringing home his catch for Antonetta to fry up for lunch.

After two years of being wrapped in the troublemaking vortex with Alli and seeing somewhat less of Lynette, Esther, and Bridgehampton, by sixteen—probably not coincidentally right after Alli got pregnant and our partying came to a halt—we original three were back together, and that summer we spent a ton of weekends in Bridgehampton. Lynette had a steady boyfriend, Rob, a sweet but tough Queens boy with a skin fade, baggy jeans, and a gold chain necklace, and since it was okay with her parents, Mark had extended an invitation for him to join us. So one Friday night, Lynette, Rob, and I piled into his little red hooptie, and in the two-hour drive from Hollis to the Hamptons, she and I prepped him.

We were on Main Street by the time we got to the part about there being no TV at Mark's, and Rob damn near crashed the car. "What!? Well, what the hell does he do at night?" Right away I thought, *We talk about the moon and the stars,* but prior to age sixteen, those conversations had mostly been reserved for just Mark and me. Suddenly I had to imagine, *Well, what if . . .* And then I panicked.

For me, the best part of talking with Mark was that he

didn't care if you were some kid unaccustomed to these sorts of discussions; he spoke and argued with you as if you were his peer, fully expecting you to keep up. And though I loved it, in that moment in the car, it occurred to me that maybe my friends wouldn't. But it was too late. There we were, pulling into the driveway.

The look on Rob's face when he first saw Mark is one that sticks with me, something like, *Holy shit. Is that a man, or is that an oak tree wearing chinos?* There was still shock on his face when they shook hands, but it softened as Mark led him toward the croquet court. "Mella and Antonetta tell me you're quite the basketball player, so I'm guessing you'll be a natural with a mallet." And for the next few hours, there they stayed, side by side on the court, one 6'10", one 6'3", one in canvas boat shoes with a popped-collar polo, one in neon Nikes with a popped-collar polo.

The day went without a hitch, but that night, after we finished dinner and moved to the pine wormwood table for dessert, I could feel my nerves start to go. Mark started swirling the cognac in his snifter. *Oh, man.* Then his chair goes tipping back. *Here it comes.* "So ..." he says, "if we were to presume we could fix all societal ills right here and now ..." And now he's teetering. "Where would you begin?"

Straightaway, my eyes lowered to my lap, then shut.

It's worth noting a few realities here. 1) For the duration of our three young lives, no one had ever asked us anything like that before—and even for me, having a decade of deep conversations with Mark under my belt, this was a new one. 2) While we might have been at an age, sixteen, where a person might be starting to think bigger picture—what you want to do for a living, etc.—we came from a world where it always felt there were essentially only two job options: cop ... not a cop. What else *could* there be? With little exception, our teachers, parents, uncles, aunts, et al. constantly touted that taking a solid city job, be that for the NYPD or the sanitation department or the post office or the department of education, was the reasonable career choice. It wasn't too tough to see that the subtext therein was that it was the *only* choice. In other words, why even bother thinking about *solving all society's ills,* when the machine needed cogs?

With my gaze still fixed on my knees, I took a long, panicked breath, but then I heard Rob say something. I looked up just as Lynette jumped in to disagree with him, and I saw Mark nodding along. I did my best to hide my relief and took a minute to feel like shit for having doubted the whole situation in the first place. Then, naturally, I jumped in, too. And just like that, yet another

moon-and-stars talk was off and running—for Rob and
Lynette it was the first of many more to come; on another
weekend, Esther would get in on the action, too.

When, starting at age twelve, the most extravagant luxuries
gradually started disappearing—limousine school pickups,
charter planes, the Riccobono parties in Bridgehampton—
I didn't notice. But, come age eighteen, a month after prom,
the very first time Mark went straight to bed after dinner in
Bridgehampton, I followed my mom into the kitchen.

"Whoa, no moon-and-stars talk? He sick or something?"

"No, dolly . . . it's not that."

"What, then?"

"Well, honey, I don't know what to say. He doesn't
want anyone to know."

"Ma. Come on!"

"Oh, God, dolly. Between me and you, business is
bad. Very bad. Has been for some time now. And he's
depressed. I've tried everything I can think of to help him,
but he won't let me, and he sure as hell won't talk to anyone else, professional or otherwise. I'm at a total loss. I'm

so sorry, dolly. I don't know what to say, except, I miss him, too."

Even though we would be missing Mark for a long time to come, that his business would never really recover, that his depression sounded the death knell for the moon-and-stars talks, nothing could take away from the fact that those earlier talks had forever changed the way my friends and I all thought of ourselves. Those conversations, alone, had made us realize that there was more to us than we knew. And for some, not all, but definitely for me, they also made you think: *Well, shit, if, a) I like talking about all these big things, and, b) The universe is infinite, then, c) There's gotta be more job options than being a cop.*

I'm sure that, without the moon-and-stars talks, I wouldn't have read that copy of *King Lear.* I wouldn't have taken AP English. I wouldn't have told my dad that the police academy wasn't right for me, and I wouldn't have applied for college, instead, to study Shakespeare.

17

Getting from my house on 253rd Street in Queens to my college in Manhattan took a forty-three-block bus ride, followed by a seventeen-stop subway ride. Getting there and *not coming back*—i.e., moving to "the City," for a Queens kid—took the herculean, cyclonic efforts of my mom, dad, grandparents, aunts, and uncles, plus anyone who ever knew them. All together, fueled purely by love and armed only with landlines, they jerry-rigged the most Rube Goldbergian web of favors and hookups, Riccobono-rendezvous-style.

Mom started the phone chain—she rang up her brother, Uncle Sal, who called a guy who used to work with my grandpa at MetLife, who called a girl who

worked for the MetLife—owned Stuyvesant Town apartments (which was then a middle-income housing complex,
dubbed by some "the White Projects"), who couldn't get
me a place straightaway but nudged my name to the top
of the waiting list. Her best guess was that it would take
six months to a year, so my uncle then reached out to his
ex-girlfriend's sister, who let me illegally sublet her apartment in the meantime.

For his part, Dad called his friend Anthony "Bootsy"
Zito, who ran his family's Italian bakery on the West Side
and was going to open a pizza joint on the East Side. Dad
got him to agree to hire me once he did, but that wouldn't
happen until September or October, so again, Mom called
Uncle Sal, who called his current girlfriend, Patty, who
called her high school friend, Ang, who could get me oc-
casional catering gigs at the company she'd worked for
starting in July. But I needed a bit of service-industry experience before I could land either job, since prior to this
I had only had summer jobs as a receptionist at a podia-
trist's office and with Dad at a frozen-bread distributor.
So Dad called his buddy who ran Connolly Station, an
Irish pub and restaurant, who hired me to bus tables starting the day after high school ended in June.

My Aunt Lucille, whom Grandma now lived with in
Westport, Connecticut, and who knew something of the

efforts it took to climb the ladder (one summer in high school she got a receptionist job on Wall Street and, without ever having gone to college, worked her way up to being a top trader) bought me a proper leather shoulder bag from a shop on Bleecker Street.

And of course Grandma herself was there to ease me into my new life in the city. Her contribution was to give me an exorbitant amount of money, every month, to clip her toenails.

"Take a fifty! That's what they charge at the place anyhow!"

"No they don't! It's fifteen, at the most——"

"What do you know from these fancy-ass salons they got around here? Take fifty, I said! Now she's a college girl she wants to talk back, *minchia!*"

Financial aid paid for 75 percent of my tuition at The New School, and my parents each chipped in to cover what remained. And, come the start of college at the end of August, with my catering job and my cheap Stuy Town apartment, I was able to cover my rent and living expenses, so long as I got a roommate—Kristy. She was going to Hunter College, plus working twice the hours that I was because she had to foot all her bills on her own. (Because *her dad* hadn't paid taxes in ten years, *she*, who deserved it most, couldn't get a dime of financial aid.)

Though I wasn't more than fifteen miles away from where I'd grown up, college felt otherworldly. Esther also wound up at The New School, and along with a handful of other kids from Planet Outer-Borough, we spent the first few weeks huddled up in the cafeteria in shock.

"Yo, it's like these kids have read every book ever written!"

"For real, I didn't think my high school was that bad, but, damn, I feel like I don't know shit!"

My first hard lesson came in our required freshman-level creative writing class: the teacher put an apple on her desk and said, "Okay, I know this will seem silly to some, but bear with me, I'm going somewhere with this—I want us to go around the room, and I want everyone to give an adjective to describe the apple." I started to sweat, and when it got close to being my turn, I bolted for the bathroom. I had heard the word *adjective* before, and, based on everyone's replies—*crimson, crisp, globular*—I thought I knew what it meant, but I wasn't 100 percent sure, and I was mortified.

The next week, after class, the teacher pulled me aside to give back my first paper. She had a plastic grocery bag in her hand, and she handed that to me, too. "Tara, you have a lot of potential, but your grammar is ... well ... not where it needs to be. This will help."

Inside the bag was an elementary-school grammar workbook. I about cried the first time I sat down to do those exercises, an eighteen-year-old, in my own apartment, paying my own bills, No. 2 pencil in hand, as if I were back in the third grade. The next semester I changed my major from Literature to Education—a worthy pursuit, no doubt, but, for me, a consolation inspired by my crushed self-esteem.

As it turned out, my bruised ego was quickly put in check by much graver matters—a week after I was given that grammar book, I got a call from Alli's little sister, hysterical because Alli had dropped off the baby at her parents' house for what was supposed to be three hours of babysitting and hadn't come back for three days.

When I had moved into the city for college, Alli had moved in with a new boyfriend in Brooklyn. When she first called me, the situation seemed great.

"Tara, I finally got myself a good man! He took me and the baby to Chuck E. Cheese, bought us both sneakers, then he got me earrings and that North Face I wanted;

he's a straight-up angel! He even pays for a babysitter, so we can go clubbing at night!"

But by the time I went for a visit, a few weeks after that call, the picture was far from rosy: the only furniture in the apartment were ripped-out bucket car seats and plastic milk crates, and, judging by the smell, it wasn't chicken soup they were cooking on the stove. The baby wasn't there—Alli had been leaving her with her parents for longer and longer stretches of time, until that one day when she just disappeared.

I was the only person who had been to Alli and her boyfriend's apartment, so her sister asked me to go try to find her. As soon as I hung up, I jetted straight out to Brooklyn. When I got there, Alli's apartment door was wide open, and the place was cleared out. She called me two days later. "Tell my parents I'm okay, but I can't be a mom right now. I just can't. I love her so much, but I'm fucked up." *Click.*

For the next six months she'd call her parents or me every few weeks so that we knew she was alive, but it would be another year before she and her boyfriend cleaned up their act and she got her daughter back.

Even if my bad grammar and badass friends set me apart from the other kids, I still had some of the more typical college experiences that year. I overheard a song in an East

Village café and wound up singing it for the salesman in Tower Records to see if he could tell me what it was— after a full minute of my doing a New York–accented impression of Tom Waits, he was cracking up, but he got it. "Step Right Up." That weekend, in the time it took me to ride the A train from the city to Broad Channel for my cousin Deanna's bridal shower at the VFW, I had listened to the whole *Small Change* album.

By my sophomore year I was using the words *hegemony* and *patriarchal* in sentences (luckily, that shit was short-lived). And then, right before Christmas 1999, I did the thing all girls like me, no matter where they're from, do in college: a girl.

Suzanne was a fine-arts student at Parsons School of Design. She had grown up ten minutes away from me, just across the city border, in the kind of Long Island suburban neighborhood that all my friends' parents had been shooting for when they left Brooklyn—the fact that they ended up in Queens was a sort of baby step in the right direction (a kind of White Flight with a layover). Likewise, Suzanne was my baby step into the world of East Village lesbianism— her parents had grown up in Queens, and we were both Italian/Irish mutts with pretty much the same accent, but she already owned a couple of Ani DiFranco albums.

She showed up to our first date on roller skates, wearing very Long Island girl–style gold lamé pants, but with a very East Village–style white vest made of feathers——she looked like a hooker and a chicken collided. I fell for her right away. And I nicknamed her "Birdie."

On our second date she introduced me to Fellini, and on our third, she decided my first Woody Allen film should be *Hannah and Her Sisters*. After that we spent every night together, and every morning before school we'd dance to Al Green's "Tired of Being Alone." I had slept with boys in high school and had loved one of them, but my love for Suzanne was unlike anything I had felt before. When she agreed to move in with me for our junior year, I knew it was time to come out to my parents.

Seeing as how Mom had been trying to tell me I was gay for almost a decade, coming out to her at nineteen was a lot more like admitting defeat than anything else. Her response was, "You see, dolly?!" *Done.* (If optimists had an extreme fundamentalist wing, my mother would be its leader. There she'd be in their propaganda videos, walking on clouds with a handful of daisies humming "Good Day Sunshine." Incredible.)

Telling Dad, it turned out, would be a lot harder than I expected.

At the same time that I had moved to Manhattan, my dad had gotten a new accounting job that required him moving to Atlanta, Georgia. When I turned nineteen and started dating Birdie, he was forty-nine and officially a white-collar guy living in the suburbs—albeit one who still carried two guns at all times and kept a picture of the Pope hung around the rearview mirror of his truck.

Despite his being a former cop, wannabe priest, staunch Catholic, Republican, when I called to tell him I was gay, I expected it to be fine, because, after all these years, he was still very good friends with several of the gay regulars from Gregory's. I guessed wrong. The second that sentence came out of my mouth—"Dad, I have a girlfriend"—he flipped out and insisted I fly to Atlanta to talk in person, "Now!" *Click.*

Three days later we got into his truck and drove, his only words being, "We're going to a hotel." Two hours passed in total silence, he and I practically motionless, the Pope swinging left and right.

Another hour, and we were on a one-lane road in the middle of the Blue Ridge Mountains. "Hotel, my ass!" I started to think. But just as I was imagining how he'd shoot me—or, worse, throw me into some "pray-the-gay-away" Jesus camp—a billboard appeared.

A woman not unlike the St. Pauli girl, with blond braids and huge, ahem, beer steins, smiled down at us. Next to her, in giant German Gothic lettering, it said: WELCOME TO HELEN, GEORGIA! A RE-CREATED ALPINE VILLAGE.

Somehow we had passed through an invisible transdimensional portal. Having been the lone car on a deeply wooded, curvy road, we were suddenly in a long line of minivans rolling through this Disneyland-bad, fake Bavarian town. Whole families wearing matching green hats adorned with feathers crammed the sidewalks. Three elderly guys wearing lederhosen played glockenspiels outside a place called Charlemagne's Kingdom. And there were windmills. Lots and lots of windmills.

This was it! As in, *this* was the place my dad chose to have the conversation of a lifetime with me.

We pulled into our parking space at the Heidi Motel—no shit—and headed right to the bar. For the first ten minutes we sat, stone-faced, drinking Johnnie Walker out of our complimentary beer steins like idiots. Then, in one fell swoop, he set out to discover if, how, and why I was gay, in a room that had not one but two cuckoo clocks.

First he blamed me. "You're confused, and you need therapy," he said.

"I need therapy?" I reply. "*I* need therapy?? There is an oompah band outside, Dad!"

He didn't laugh. And we spent the next six hours drinking Scotch and rehashing every argument, disagreement, and previously unexamined minuscule moment of contention we'd had in my nineteen years of life. From the time Tommy O'Reilly knocked me blind to when I stuck pencil erasers into my ears and he took me to the doctor thinking I was going deaf, from the time he told me not to play in the grass in my Easter dress, so I climbed the tree instead, from how he used to hide all my presents at the O'Reillys', since we didn't have any closets in the boat shed, and when I woke up on Christmas morning, there would be 360 degrees of toys all around me on our pullout sofa bed, to the countless, mind-numbing hours he spent watching me try on sneakers, from my notorious asphalt head dive, all the way to how furious he was at me for getting into so much trouble in high school and for drifting away from him.

Then, if for only a few seconds, he went from blaming me to blaming himself. "I shouldn't have bought you those G.I. Joes when you were a kid! Or the Hot Wheels."

And then he got quiet and said to himself as much as to me, "What did I know about bringing up a girl? I just did what I could," and, a second time, even softer, "I just did what I could."

And then he hugged me—for as long as a pick-up-the-guns/three *S*'s/red-light-running/mustache-and-aviator-glasses kind of guy does. And I hugged him back—for as long as a G.I. Joe–collecting/high-tops-wearing/head-down-on-asphalt-diving/Tom Waits–listening kind of lesbian does. And with that, we broke for dinner, across the street at Heidelberg's Schnitzelhaus.

We made small talk. It was still a bit tense, but Heidelberg's Schnitzelhaus is a hard place to stay angry (in addition to the lederhosen-clad waiters and the oompah band soundtrack, the place was strung from end to end with garlands of triangular German flags uniquely interspersed with hanging plastic Bavarian pretzels). Dad confessed that he had asked his new coworkers where to spend the weekend with his visiting teenage daughter. Of course, he'd neglected to mention the nature of the visit and was as shocked as I was when we had arrived in Helen.

Then, somewhere in between the sauerbraten and the strudel, my dad surrendered. He looked up, raised his glass, and said, "Ah, screw it. At least now we have two things in common—whiskey and women!"

18

You only live once, but if you do it right, once is enough.

—Mae West

Grandma told me she was going to croak every month for two years before she actually did—I'd come to cut her toenails, and within minutes she'd scream, "I'm gonna croak, you know! Probably soon. So you'd better get ready!" Then we'd crack up.

She died on February 9, 2000, three months before my twentieth birthday. I was home alone at my apartment in Stuy Town, and Mom was home in Queens. She got the news first, of course, but she was such a wreck, both with her own grief and at the thought of having to tell me, that my cousin Danny ended up being the first to call that day, presuming I already knew.

"Yo, T, you okay?"

"Yeah, why?"

"Oh, shit . . ."

"What!?"

"I thought you—"

"What?!!"

"Shit!"

"Don't—"

"I'm coming over. Shit, just wait—"

"No. No! Oh, no . . . oh, please. Oh—"

And then my knees gave out. And the phone went flying. And I cried longer and harder than I have ever cried before or since.

The last words I spoke to my grandmother were "I love you." The last words she spoke to me, in reply, were, "Come closer. Closer, *che cazzo!* I have to tell you something, a secret. In an eyeglass case, in my purse, in the back of the closet, not here, at Lucille's, is a hundred-dollar bill I hid. Take it!" Then I kissed her cheek and walked out of the nursing home, and a week later she was gone.

Her funeral Mass was held back in Brooklyn, at Our

Lady of Peace, the same church where she had had her baptism, First Communion, Confirmation, and wedding. And she was buried at Green-Wood Cemetery, alongside her parents, brothers, my grandfather, and my Great-aunt Grapefruits, her beloved sister Mary.

I took two weeks off from school, and when I returned, I was a disaster, but I muscled through the end of that semester and decided to take the following one off, but not before changing my major back to Literature and signing up for a paid internship that summer at the Shakespeare Theatre of New Jersey.

It wasn't until a month after her death that I remembered what she had told me on that last visit. She had been pretty sick, and her memory had been all screwy for months, but I went to my aunt's house to look anyway. And in that purse, way back in the closest, in an otherwise empty eyeglass case, was that fucking hundred-dollar bill—best laugh I had had for a long time.

Birdie and I road-tripped to New Orleans at the end of that summer after my internship. We made a stop in Virginia, where Great-uncle Jelly had since moved, to a condo crammed with birdcages, vases, and what looked like half the furniture from his old antiques shop in upstate New

York. He brought out some old pictures and showed us one of a teenage Grandma, in a bikini, draped over the hood of a Model-T Ford. Then he told us a story of how, just before she got married, Grandma talked about singing in nightclubs, like her hero Mae West, and he wondered if she regretted never giving it a whirl. It was the first I'd ever heard of it.

On the drive from Virginia to Georgia to visit Dad, Birdie convinced me to try another writing class.

I balked for my first semester in junior year, but by the second I worked up the guts to sign up for Playwriting 101. The first scene I wrote was a word-for-word account of one of my last conversations with Grandma:

TARA ARRIVES TO CUT GRANDMA'S TOENAILS.

    Grandma
Minchia! Look who decides to finally come over here! I just said, if this kid don't show up soon, the nails are gonna come through my socks!

    Tara
I been nuts. School, work—you know. Sorry—

    Grandma
Okay, enough! You ready?

    Tara
Yeah, gimme your foot . . .

> Grandma
Good. Cos we gotta talk about
something . . .

> Tara
What?

> Grandma
X-mas balls.

> Tara, now looking up from Grandma's
> feet
What??

> Grandma
In the garage . . . in a box.

> Tara
It's July—whattaya want with Christmas
balls?

> Grandma
You're not listening! See? Just like
when you were a kid! X-MAS BALLS. X-MAS
BALLS! There's no Christmas balls in the
box.

> Tara
I really don't know what the hell you're
talkin' about now.

> Grandma
Madonna! Then listen! In the box what
says X-M-A-S-B-A-L-L-S is all my good
jewelry.

> Tara
Why? Other foot.

Grandma

Whattaya mean, why? So the crooks don't get it, that's why! When I moved here, from Queens, I put it there. I figured your fancy aunt with all her fancy stuff in her fancy house would make the robbers come! I put it there so they wouldn't get it. I figured what would a bunch of crooks want with Christmas balls anyway? Nothing! They don't care about no Christmas!

Anyhow, now you know.

EPILOGUE

It's a beautiful spring day, blue skies, sunshine, ten o'clock in the morning, and I am in a bar—the kind of bar that, well, opens at ten o'clock in the morning. All right, so it's not the Ritz, but it's mine. It's my family's bar in the West Village, the one owned by Uncle Sal, where my mother worked when she was younger, and now that I'm twenty-one, I work here, too. I am a bartender and a senior in college.

On this particular morning, there are only two people in the bar: myself and a regular named Joe Bird. Now, Joe was from South Boston (*Good Will Hunting*–type South Boston, Mark Wahlberg South Boston). He always wears jeans and a flannel shirt and work boots, and I've known him for years, but I don't know what he does for a living. I've kind of presumed he's in construction, but he never offers, and I never ask. He comes in and drinks Budweiser, nothing but Budweiser, and never short of a case, with or without the help of his younger brother, Danny (worse drunk, better teeth). But on this day Danny isn't here; today it's just Joe and me.

The bar has its ups and downs; on the upside, business is really good, because we have a lot of regulars. And on the downside, *business is really good, because we have a lot of regulars.* In fact, we have so many that, just like back at Gregory's, we give them nicknames to set them apart: We've got Big Joe, because he's big, and Black Joe, because he's black, and One-Arm Joe, because he actually only has one arm. Then there are a few guys who got their nicknames based on the kind of work they did: Jimmy Ice Cream sold ice cream, and Vinnie the Fish sold fish. And, we have so many guys named Eddie that one of them is called Goiter Eddie. The giant goiter under his chin isn't his only accessory; he also has an oxygen tank that he drags into the bar behind him, day after day—I'm not sure who decided we should call him Goiter Eddie over Oxygen Tank Eddie.

Now, obviously, there was a lot more to these guys than their jobs or their goiters, but because they didn't go around spouting their life stories, even though people didn't know the first thing about them, they judged. And when I say "people," I mean me.

At this point, I'm still kind of this little shit—I got the college walk, the college talk, and I'm not yet past overusing the word *polemic*. And here I am, sitting across from Joe, and he's reading the *Post*, I'm reading the *Times* (schmuck), and he looks up from his paper and says, "You see this, kid? Looks like they really are going to ban smoking in bars." And I say, "I guess that's what you call cultural hegemony." And he says, "I guess that's what you call—WHAT THE HELL are you talking about??"

Come noon, Joe's still drinking Buds, and I've ordered myself some Chinese food for lunch. The delivery guy hands me the bill, and right away I see that I've been overcharged, and so I say as much, pretty nicely. But he doesn't understand—he's not a native English speaker, and, between how fast I talk and my accent, in some ways, neither am I—but I've been charged for two orders of dumplings instead of one, so I try to pay what I actually owe, and he gets pissed and points to the amount on the bill, and I try to open the bag to see if there's actually two orders in there to show him, and he grabs the bag away and gives me the *pay-up* hand, and I get pissed, and words aren't working, and now we're just yelling, and the bag is going back and forth, and before you know it, we're playing tug-of-war with a carton of pork fried rice … and that's when Joe stands up.

Joe being Joe, when he slides in between us, I figure he's just gonna coldcock this dude, and without thinking, I shut my eyes. But what I hear next shoots them right back open—Joe Bird is speaking slowly and calmly … and completely in Chinese.

This guy, who just an hour ago was drinking a bottle of Bud and eating a bag of Fritos for breakfast, this guy, whom I have known for years and years, his only notable change being a little more or a little less pee on his pants, THIS GUY is rattling on and on in fluent Chinese! What's more, it seems that he and the delivery guy are patching things up; they're patting each other on the back, and they're doing that "Everything's cool, bro" IN CHINESE, and then the guy trots on out, and Joe sits back at the bar and takes a sip of his beer as if nothing ever happened.

I'm now in a state of shock. All I can do is stare at him. I can't speak. But finally, thankfully, Joe does. He says, just as nonchalantly as if he were asking for another Bud, "I sell pigeons."

My mouth says nothing; my eyebrows say, *What the fuck???*

He goes on. "A couple of years back I expanded the

business to Hong Kong, and you know, my brother, he doesn't speak Cantonese, and it *really* holds him back!"

Nope. I still got nothing.

"Listen, I know it's weird, but my father started the business years ago, and it was all just an accident."

That does it. "Joe!" I say. "How the hell do you accidentally sell a pigeon?!"

And with that, we both shut our newspapers and slide them to the side, knowing there's nothing in there that's gonna be better than this.

"So maybe forty, fifty years ago my father was driving through Boston in a pickup loaded with cages of his racing pigeons. He stops at a light in Chinatown, and a woman approaches and asks him the price. He's caught off guard. He explains that he trains his pigeons himself, and no one has ever asked to buy one before, but she cuts him off and explains that she doesn't want to race them, she wants to *eat* them."

(And, hey, to all of you who just made that face: people eat pigeon all over the world! Even here in New York City, at white-tablecloth joints, they call it "squab" and charge you thirty dollars.)

Joe continues. "So my dad goes home that night, and he really thinks about it, and a little lightbulb goes off— street pigeons!"

"Street pigeons?"

"Yup, street pigeons. They are talentless, but they are edible! And, more important, they're free—no overhead, tons of supply, BINGO! The family business was born! All I did was take it to the next level. Started exporting, you know—"

I interrupt. "Take it to the next level? Joe, man, you're a mogul! It's like, like, what McDonald's did for the hamburger, you've done for the street pigeon!"

Now, of course, all of this is completely illegal, which is why Joe and his brother had kept it a secret. And so, what's the point? The point is that I was an idiot, and for two reasons. One, up until this very moment I had thought that Bird was his real last name. And, two, here I was working in *my* family business but thinking I was ambitious, acting as if I was better than all these "bar people" I had grown up with just because I was in college, only to find out that these "bar people" had actually taught themselves Cantonese to be secret, international, criminal pigeon dealers! How's that for ambition?

Afterward, since his secret was out of the bag, I got to know Joe a bit better. He invited me to his apartment one day, and it was incredible—there were a half dozen jade Buddhas and tons of beautiful, antique, bamboo furniture. And one night, when I ran into him on the street, he showed me how to catch a street pigeon. You have to do this one fluid motion in a split second: you walk up to a pigeon, maybe a foot away or so, and you stomp, they fly, you clap—*bam!* Pigeon. Sounds easy . . . but it ain't.

It's been over ten years since I last ran into Joe Bird. There's as much of a chance that he's OD'ed as there is that he's now heading a department for Google.

It has also been over a decade since that night in Bridgehampton when I first caught wind of Mark's business's fatal collapse. The cause of which really just boiled down to two things: hard luck and the fact that anyone born to booze and grease simply isn't given a safety net and rarely learns to build one.

Mark's resulting depression never fully let up, and it would one day claim the life of his relationship with my mother. Afterward, due in large part to Mom's strong encouragement, me and other Riccobonos kept in touch with our beloved *Mastagotz.* We stayed in contact until his death, when he was in his eighties, just a few weeks after

I started writing this book—for which he gave his proud blessing.

As for me, though it was certainly Mark and our moon and stars talks that first stretched the horizons of my thinking, it took Joe Bird, and the lessons of time, to forever alter the way I look at people, including myself.

A year after I learned Joe's story, I was bartending again, at 10:00 a.m., and again there was only one guy in the bar; a different regular, sitting on the last stool by the window. Outside the window there's a guy walking to work. He's got a briefcase, and he's wearing a suit, and he's staring in as he passes. My regular is staring right back. I'm looking at them looking at each other . . . and for the first time I realize that they're both thinking the exact same thing: *poor guy*.

ACKNOWLEDGMENTS

Domenica Alioto. DO-MEN-I-CA AL-I-O-TO. Despite having such an ungodly number of syllables in her name that someone might think she was one of my great many Italian relatives, she is not—she is the editor of this book. And yet, our lack of shared DNA notwithstanding, she has become family to me.

Turning the grammatically incorrect ramblings of a headstrong Queens girl into a legible book takes more than editorial skill; it takes planting yourself on a bar-stool and listening to her stories, sitting shotgun in her old Honda driving around the ass-end of Queens, and spending hour after hour on the phone with a person who was somehow, simultaneously, both super-insecure about her ability to write a book at all and yet so defensive, she wasn't easy to talk into making changes. It takes earning said asshole's trust. It takes a gift that I'm pretty damn sure is only possessed by one supremely dedicated and intelligent woman with an eight-syllable name. In other words, if you liked this book, then know that the credit is as much Domenica's as mine. And if you didn't, well, what can I say . . . she gave it her best.

Anna Stein, Robert Strent, Howie Sanders, and Peter Gethers are my alternate universe version of a Queens handball court crew—thank you all!

By pure luck I crossed paths several years ago with Lauren Cerand, and her support was what ultimately got this whole writing thing started for me. I'm forever grateful, lady.

Huge—or should I say, 'uge—thanks to everyone at the Moth for letting me tell my stories on your stage and radio show, and for being such lovely and supportive people. Thanks also to John McElwee, Alex Hoyt, Michael Ferrante, and Honor Jones, for editing several of my previously published stories. And I'm enormously grateful to Michael Howard for reading the very first draft of this book and making one helluva call!

Without Kel O'Neill this book might never have been started; and without Robert Voris it most certainly wouldn't have been finished. And much love to Suzanne and Blake Ashman-Kipervaser, Whitney Estrin, David Goodman, Tiffany Brightman, Holly Ivey, Kate Glass, Rich Neuwirth, Gail Thomas, Sal "Papa" Schifilliti, Jackie and Colby Clancy, and Christine Ponton.

I'm also very grateful to my whole Crown crew: Claire Potter, Terry Deal, Dyana Messina, Liz Esman, Danielle Crabtree, Chris Brand, Songhee Kim, Matt Inman, Donna Passannante, Annsley Rosner, and Molly Stern.

There are no composite characters or pseudonyms in this book. And that all of the following people allowed me to use their real names and tell their stories is an honor second only to my being able to call them my best friends:

Esther and Lynette, our friendship is one of the greatest gifts of my life. You are my sisters. L.E.T. crew, forever.

Al, I love you, girl. Did I just put that in print? Hell yeah, I did! So maybe you can wait five minutes after reading this before texting me some chop-busting shit about how I've gone soft, and just take it in.

Birdie, where would I be without your crazy brilliant ass? You're my favorite roller-skating, Snooki-looking, soccer-whiz, arty hooker/chicken in the world!

Kristy—thanks for accompanying me on the long and arduous journey from Queens to Manhattan. You're amazing.

Antonetta, Jen, Johanna, and John Solina, Phyllis Silverman, and Rob Hauer are family . . . period.

And special thanks to the O'Reillys, Rosemary Gallagher, all of my teammates on the St. Gregory the Great softball team, all of the regulars and staff of Gregory's Bar and Restaurant and Barrow's Pub (most especially, Joe Bird), and each and every one of my not-so-small army of blood relations, the Clancys and the Riccobonos.

My wife, Shauna Lewis, is the world's sexiest saint, and without her this book couldn't have been written. And, our sons, Ray and Harry, fill me with more joy than hitting all the buttons on all the Overhead Control Panels in all the world. Thank you a million times, my dears.

Dad, thanks for being the greatest storyteller I know, for the unwavering love, and for always letting me eat the dessert first on a TV dinner. I love you so very much, and I'm proud to be your daughter.

And to my mom, my best friend, I can't think of any other way to put it than to say: you are the most beautiful human being I've ever met. I'm the luckiest schmuck in the world to have you for a mother. Thank you. Thank you. Thank you.

Acknowledgments

In Loving Memory:

Tina and Lenny Curranci, Anna and Joe Paradise, Alice, Gilbert Sr., Gilbert, Arthur, Thomas, and Dennis Clancy, Margaret Merkle, Guilio Portobello, and Mary Zacchio.

Josh Miller, I miss you so much, my friend. You were the linchpin.

Bruno Riccobono, what I wouldn't give to steal one more used tennis ball with you . . .

Mark Ponton, you changed my life. I'll love you always, *Mastagotz.*

And to the boss-lady herself, my hero, Rosalie *"Che cazzo!"* Riccobono, here's hoping you're in heaven, telling everyone to fuck off.

See previous 250 or so pages.